LIFE FROM DEATH EMERGING

Paul Bradbury works for Oak Tree Anglican Fellowship in Acton, west London, where he runs a community project called The New Hope Project. He has at various times been a teacher in Africa, a youth worker in Glasgow, a research scientist with the Medical Research Council and a strategic planner for The Children's Society. He is married to Emily and has two children. This is his first book.

Life from Death Emerging

Paul Bradbury

TRIANGLE

Published in Great Britain in 2002
Triangle
SPCK
Holy Trinity Church
Marylebone Road
London NW1 4DU

British Library Cataloguing-in-Publication Data

A catalogue record for this book is available from the British
Library

ISBN 0-281-05458-4

Typeset by Trinity Typing, Wark-on-Tweed
Printed in Great Britain by Omnia Books, Glasgow

Subsequent digital printing in Great Britain by Cambridge University Press

Contents

For Emily

*Proceeds from the sale of this book will be donated to the
Cystic Fibrosis Trust.*

The CF Trust is the only national charity solely concerned
with the well-being of people with CF. It provides practical
support for families coping with relatives with CF and
fundraising for medical research to find a cure.

CF Trust: 020 8464 7211
www.cftrust.org.uk

Acknowledgements

I would like to thank the many people who have assisted me in the thought process that paralleled the writing of this book, notably the Revd James Blandford-Baker, Geoff and Caroline Nicholson, Sarah Towers and Susan Hauser. I am indebted to the Revd Mike Lloyd for much of the theology that helped formulate my thinking on Chapter 2.

Most of all I would like to thank my wife Emily for her willingness to see this book written, her support during its creation and her deep wisdom and sensitivity towards the personal nature of its subject.

Introduction

On a bleak, grey day in late December I witnessed with my own eyes the visible bright beginnings of a new life. After some 12 hours in a rather stark and uninspiring hospital room this unfurling life emerged into the arms of a midwife and blinked with shock and fear at the bright world as we greeted him. A squashed, purple, anxious-looking little person, he was handed to my wife, Emily, and we gathered round him and cried with joy.

We had made it. After nine months of the usual joy, anxiety, anticipation and fear, we had arrived. He had arrived, and our lives, our two existences, would now remain radically changed forever by the addition of a new life.

Jacob was our first child. We felt young to be having children. Most of our contemporaries were barely married, let alone considering children. We were on an adventure into this extraordinary world of parenthood relatively alone, and while we had no pretension about the challenges that suggested, the moment that Jacob was born felt like the end of the road, an arrival rather than a departure.

Preparing for a baby focuses the mind on one thing – the birth itself. Endless antenatal classes on pain relief, birth positions, breathing, massage and other minutiae of the great event left us over-prepared for the birth and completely unprepared for the aftermath. There is no doubt that for everyone a first child, the arrival of this rather sedentary, at times noisy, but otherwise unassuming human being is the doorway into a new world. That new world opens before us in ways we would never have expected, never predicted.

Perhaps it is no wonder we focus in on the birth; it is on one level hard to prepare for the rest. Because somehow we feel different. We certainly have to live differently. And we know that somehow life will never be the same again.

For everyone having children requires an adjustment, whether it's returning to work or readapting to life as a full-time parent, or simply getting used to life without lie-ins, without time to be quiet and uninterrupted, without the freedom to jump in the car and go out at a moment's notice. We are no longer our own sole agents: someone else begins to invade our time and priorities. But we do adjust, and at some point down the road we muse nostalgically at life without children while being thankful for the joy and benefits children bring.

Somehow for us it was different. The arrival of Jacob had an impact far beyond that of most children. Not because he was any more special, or that we were particularly sensitive to his arrival or in need of wholesale change in order to cope with his existence – but because he was sick. Jacob really 'arrived' a little later that we expected, perhaps even nine months later. His journey and our journey with him was a journey from that initial birth, backwards then forwards, down and then up. Backwards and downwards into the realms of death, then forwards and upwards back into life.

Alongside that incredible journey of life and death was a parallel journey of faith. There is a theory of evolution that supposes that organisms do not evolve at some fixed pace in a long gradual upwards curve through time from least evolved to most. Rather, certain external conditions, usually environmental, act to enforce periods of rapid evolution, diversification and adaptation. The path of evolution is thus a series of steps rather than a gentle slope. Whether or not you agree with this theory, indeed whether you subscribe to the theory of evolution at all, this model provides a powerful metaphor for what happened to us – what happens to all of us in our faith when things get tough enough to challenge the very basis of our faith. Like living organisms, tough conditions, situations or passages of time that challenge our lives to the very core are times, in terms of faith, of do or die. We evolve, develop, rethink, repent and move on, or we fall away, our faith overcome by the sheer enormity of what faces us.

This is surely one of the great paradoxes of the Christian faith. For while in one case suffering strengthens, in another it undermines. While many argue that suffering makes them find a loving God hard to imagine, let alone believe in, for others it is the thing that redefined and reinvigorated their faith. Is suffering therefore 'a megaphone to wake a deaf world', as C. S. Lewis said so often? Or is it simply what so many people think, the harsh reality of a godless world, out of control and random – or worse than that, the consequence of a malicious and cynical deity with a megalomaniacal bent.

While this book is a book about suffering it is not a book *about* suffering. In other words, this book does not attempt to argue one way or the other about the place of suffering in a God-created world or otherwise. Rather it is a book of two stories. First, of Jacob and of Bethany. Not long after he was born Jacob became very sick, and underwent lots of tests. He was misdiagnosed, then diagnosed with cystic fibrosis, and spent nearly two months in hospital. At the age of seven months he finally came home from hospital for good. Before she was even conceived, Bethany, our second child, faced a one in four chance of inheriting the same life-threatening disease we knew Jacob to have. Second, it is the story of their relatively young fragile human parents and of the insights, reflections and journeys of faith that the experience of suffering generated in those same people.

Ultimately it is a real-life story. Not in the rather crass, sensationalist, tabloid sense, but in the sense of an attempt to earth what often becomes a rather abstract theology of God and suffering. It tells the story of what happens when two Christian people, with an evangelical background imbued with a clear belief in a victorious and ultimately good God, are faced with a situation that suggests only defeat and the absence of that same God.

Too often we live our Christian faith at the extremes of a spectrum, either in the triumphalistic surroundings of a very present heaven, as though we had already obtained salvation to the full, or in the pessimistic environment of an earth devoid of divine intervention, going through the motions of Christian commitment in a desperate attempt to secure salvation for ourselves at the end of the day. The scary and yet more real thing is to dare to live somewhere in the middle: somewhere in the tension between ultimate death and ultimate life. In doing so we may just discover what death is really about, and similarly life. So few of us dare to do that, and when tough times come we are ill-prepared. And yet the truth is, that's where we all are, stuck between death and life, darkness and light, with a taste of heaven tantalizingly on our lips but the repeating discomfort of death in our stomach.

Hopefully this story of two stories will dare people to explore the space in between, the shadowland in the gap between the cross and the return of Christ, between the darkened glass and the clarity of the apocalypse. This is our challenge, day by day, to live in two worlds, holding them in tension. It is a tough, sometimes dangerous thing to do. It frequently suggests the hard option, or the illogical option. It leads us through deeper depths, confronts us with things we would more naturally leave alone, yet it promises an experience of life that is 'full', here and now.

Barometer Readings

Rage, rage against the coming of the night
                                    Dylan Thomas

~I~

Before you were, I formed
Your arrival in terms of flowers;
Bursting inflorescences, camomile lawns
Deserts blooming after sharp showers,
Vibrancy, sudden and arresting.
But you took your time to bloom,
Lying closed tight shut soon
After the fluorescent
Bands and self-assuring bleeps
Had ceased, blood flowed,
And the life that starts tomorrow
Finally drawn closer.

                    You didn't sleep.

And that night in a far away desert it rained
Solid drops bulleting the earth like nails.

~1~

The Meaning of 'Life'

In the beginning God created ...

Genesis 1.1

I have come in order that you may have life – life in all its fullness.

John 10.10, GNB

And that is precisely what Christianity is about. This world is a great sculptors shop. We are the statues and there is a rumour that some of us are some day going to come to life.

C. S. Lewis[1]

It took me some time to get used to the idea of having a child, and being a father. About a week after discovering that my wife Emily was pregnant, I found myself having to wait on a pavement as a long line of primary schoolchildren, paired up and hand in hand, crossed the road in front of me. I stood gawping incredulously as though they were penguins, or alien visitors, not human beings. The very idea that one of these living, breathing creatures was just going to appear out of nowhere, and that it could grow up to call me 'Dad' was both unbelievable and ridiculous.

After the initial phase of denial I did eventually join in with the whole process of pregnancy. I went to scans, which showed a perfectly formed baby wriggling around inside Emily in extraordinary detail, even to the extent of seeing the veins running through a tiny leg and a delicate heart beating like a pocket watch. I went to a series of antenatal classes on every possible aspect of the birth process and to further classes on how to help my wife get through the ordeal of giving birth.

It struck me in all this preparation that perhaps the modern British man is not quite the stiff upper-lipped stoic he was once caricatured to be. In particular, the British man at the birth of his child is no longer the finger-chewing, chain-smoking occupant of the hospital waiting room. On the contrary, the new British man is present and involved, eager to experience the extraordinary event of a life beginning.

I was no different. The ambient assumption from all around me was that the birth of our child was something I shouldn't miss. People talked passionately, even evangelistically, about the importance of being there. My wife wanted me, indeed needed me, to be there, and apart from that there were benefits for me – an experience that, according to many, would change my life in a quite radical way.

In some ways this is something of a relief. It illustrates a renewed awareness that there is something more to life than simply the matter that comprises us. What we seem to be rediscovering, at the end of one highly materialistic century and the beginning of another, is that the origin of matter, and the origin of our very selves, is not as self-evident as some would have us think. Seeing as none of us was actually present to experience how we ourselves came to exist, the best we can do is stand aghast as a life very close to ours comes into being. We are rediscovering mystery. We are at last rediscovering that all of life cannot be reduced to atoms, or any other infinitesimal minutiae of matter. When any father stands present, as I did, to watch his child become visible to his own eyes in a rush of fluid and blood, in what seems a fraction of a second, is to connect in some way with the unanswerable questions of creation and being.

So I was there, and at the end of the day, as I drove home from a hospital where a new life lay next to an exhausted mother, I had few rational thoughts going through my head. Instead I only had thoughts of wonder and awe, thoughts bordering on the mystic, touching the mysterious and the spiritual.

Life is an enigmatic mixture, that we seem intent on distilling and experimenting into a simple and understand-able form. We are told that essentially we are all, in our being and our behaviour, the products of the genetic material in each constituent cell. Or we are simply random forms of matter flung together for a short time, a small step in evolution's march to ever greater levels of sophistication. Either way, we seem intent on reducing life to an equation with a solution, or to a diagram with a set of neat measurements against an appropriate scale. However, the rumour that we are something more has never been put to rest. It finds its way to the surface of our experience at various times in our lives, sometimes even when we do not seek it – such as the birth of a child.

Birth is more and more becoming a quasi-spiritual experience. The way we approach the process of birth reflects this. Birth has become a potentially religious rite of passage for the mother. A generation ago mothers were transported into hospital at the mere inkling of the beginnings of birth and they could expect to stay in for a week before finally returning home with a baby. Birth was seen as a medical event and was treated as such. Now, more and more we seek to find room to explore the transcendent experience of birth. The environment of birth has increasingly moved from the hospital to the home, so that the mother can get closer to this extraordinarily natural and revealing process.

For us, all our plans for something nearing a natural birth were quickly dispelled when Emily's waters broke. A green colouring in the fluid immediately meant that we were beckoned into hospital for observation. The time that followed, between entering hospital and the final delivery, was a very clinical experience. Emily was put on a drip and had a foetal heart monitor attached to her abdomen. Her contractions were monitored for the entirety of her labour. A rather bleak and starkly furnished delivery room was filled for 12 hours with the signature tune of hospitals, a steady bleeping accompanied by various flashing lights.

In our experience then, the emergence of this new life was scientifically managed throughout. Scarcely had he taken his first breath and been allowed to cry that joyous cry of arrival,

Jacob was being attended to by a fiercely professional paediatrician who sought to ensure that none of the poisonous green fluid, called meconium, remained in his lungs. Jacob had a very managed arrival. There seemed less room than we had expected for communing with the source of life itself or enjoying a sense of intimacy with creation and the Creator. Yet this experience of birth only served to demonstrate man's rather ambiguous approach to the dawning of life. It is either clinical and scientific or vaguely spiritual. There does not, or at least did not for us, seem to be some kind of middle ground that sought some explanation for the conflict between these two extremes.

Yet it is impossible, even for those who have had birth experiences more clinical than our own, to avoid the fact that there is great mystery inherent to the process of life and creating life. We ourselves emerge from the process of bringing a child into being with many questions and few answers; all our thoughts and emotions are a faint and rather poor attempt by our feeble minds to come to terms with an unnatural, even supernatural, event. No wonder we call birth a miracle.

This apparent contradiction – for us, between the clinical process of birth and the gentle wonder of a sleeping baby, for others, between a reasoned philosophy of life and an experience that seems to outstrip the boundaries of that same reason – is worth exploring. It is important to talk about life and what we might mean by it, before we can begin to talk about what we tend to use as shorthand for its absence, death. Life, after all, is one of those words we bandy about with huge liberty and we seldom stop to think what on earth we might mean.

Life in all its fullness?
Jesus makes an extraordinary statement, which John records. He says that he has come that we might have life 'in all its fullness' (John 10.10, GNB). Funny that only after our experience of life and death with our first child have I come to re-examine that statement. For like the word 'life', this statement

has a self-evident quality to it. For the initiated it surely means that Jesus has come to enable us to enter into heaven, to come into a new transcendent quality of existence summed up in that phrase 'fullness of life'. This is true. When Jesus says in the same passage, 'I am the gate; whoever enters through me will be saved. He will come in and go out and find pasture' (John 10.9), he is making one of those unambiguous statements about who he is. He is the way to the Father, the key to eternal life, he is the gateway to heaven.

And that is generally how we envision it in our minds. In my mind there is the stereotypical image of some misty celestial vista the other side of that gate, with a gleaming whiteness to it brighter than eyes can bear. It is a transcendent place, removed from our earthly experience, and Jesus stands at the gate and beckons us in. 'Life to the full', then, is based in this kind of arena, 'the other side'. Not here in the grubby experience of earth where thieves and robbers do indeed steal and kill and destroy. Heaven is another place, eternal life a future experience, life to the full something waiting on the other side of the gate.

'Life to the full', in this perspective, is code for utopia: a heavenly place we can only dream of. It is formed in our minds from the longings for a place free from the harsh realities of theft, death and destruction and full of the sort of peaceful and generally rural images that Jesus employs. Small wonder, then, that writers over the centuries have written about their own utopias, from Thomas More writing in the sixteenth century, who described a place where there was no poverty or luxury and where there was justice and peace, to modern writers such as Julian Barnes, who described heaven as a place where grapefruits didn't squirt in your eye and every round of golf was played out in 18 shots.

Unfortunately our western conception of sheep and shepherds does not help. We usually think of shepherds as gentle, almost effeminate men living close to their cuddly and quiet flocks. We think of the shepherding life as calm, peaceful and somehow trouble free. However, even a rudimentary exploration of first-century shepherding in Judea unearths something of the profundity of what Jesus is saying. Shepherding was a tough business and a very dangerous one. Typically sheep would be herded into a common pen for the night and a group of owners would club together to hire a watchman to look after the flock for the night. No doubt thieves and bandits were a concern, otherwise Jesus would not have used the image. So a single watchman was expected to protect the sheep from such attackers. Pasture was not easy to find and shepherds would lead their flocks considerable distances to find pasture. In doing so they were vulnerable to various preying animals, such as the wolves that Jesus mentions. Shepherding was indeed a risky vocation and a shepherd dedicated to his task had to be strong, brave and self-sacrificial.

None of this disappears in Jesus' metaphor at the moment that he talks about 'life in all its fullness'. We are not suddenly transported out of the tough and very real environment that his hearers would have found so familiar. This is the backdrop not only for the place where thieves and robbers come to steal and destroy but also for the 'life in all its fullness' that he invites us to. The sheep come in through the gate and receive it, but then they 'come in and go out, and find pasture'. Do they go out to a wolf-free pasture? No, but they are led carefully and diligently, and find pasture rather than being run ragged by wolves because of a careless shepherd who thinks of himself rather than his flock. So even a cursory examination of the basis for Jesus' statement reveals that 'life in all its fullness' is not the straightforward benefit or realm of existence that perhaps we imagine in our mind. Life in all its fullness and the humdrum, grubby existences of the world are not either side of the fence. They exist side by side. They are parallel worlds that are separated not by tangible things such as concrete, fences or gates but by more slippery things such as attitude, love, commitment and care.

Fundamentally Jesus' 'life in all its fullness' is all around us. It is not waiting on the other side when we die, with a benevolent Jesus standing at the gate waiting to usher us gratefully in. It is in the here and now, and we are invited to experience it if we want to.

In birth, and in modern approaches to it by average normal human beings searching for meaning, we are actually proving that fact. Life is not just the clinical and the scientific, even this side of heaven. There is something more, and instinctively we all know it and struggle after it in various fashion. Something within us tells us that when life is stripped down to its constituent parts – when a person lies on the floor in bits, atoms and molecules piled on top of one another – what we look down upon is not all there is. We are most definitely more than the sum of all our parts. Something about seeing those infinitely complicated and marvellous parts come into being before our very eyes, functioning, breathing and capable of life, tells us that this has to be true.

The physical and the spiritual
C. S. Lewis makes a key distinction in this quest for an understanding of life. There is something to be learnt, he says, from knowing the difference between making and begetting. When something is made it is by definition different from the person that made it. I make a chair or a cake, things which are obviously very different in form from me who made them. When something is begotten, however, it is like that which made it. It looks like them, has characteristics like them, perhaps feels and acts like them. In seeing something that is begotten, we perhaps have an inkling of who was the begetter. God made the heavens and the earth but he begets Jesus his son. Jesus was, as the Nicene Creed states, 'begotten not made'. In Jesus we see God the Father. In the same way I beget Jacob, my son, and sometimes people see me in him; they certainly see much of his mother in him. As he grows up it will become more and more apparent to people that I am the father of Jacob and he is my son.

Why is this distinction so important? It is important because it helps us make sense of the apparent ambiguity in our approaches to life. It helps us understand why a proud and generally unemotional father can be reduced to tears at the sight of his newborn child. It helps us understand why the inexorable progress of science can appear to squeeze the very life out of life. For in making and begetting we have two forms of life with one origin, God, yet they are substantially different. Lewis uses two different Greek words to describe them. For the made world, the created world that forms the basis of life on this planet, he uses the word *bios*. This is the earthy stuff. The basic ingredients. For the other form of life, the life that is begotten, he uses the word *zoe*. This is essentially the Greek word that encapsulated the spiritual realm, the transcendent realm, the realm of God and of the supernatural.

These two words describe what life is about. For life is not just about one or the other. Life is not just about *bios* – the physical matter that constitutes the ground beneath our feet, the air we breathe and the matter we consist of. But nor, evidently, is life simply spiritual and ethereal. We cannot even go out the door at the beginning of the day without recognizing that our existence is dependent on tangible things, things of matter such as the body we have, the clothes we wear and the ground at our feet. And while few have fallen foul of ditching matter in favour of the spiritual to any great acclaim or success, we are spectacularly adept at ditching all that is spiritual and making out that matter is all there is. We do it all the time. Even those of us who consider ourselves spiritual people.

Before Jacob was born, or even considered, I thought I had a pretty good grasp of what life was about. As a scientist I understood matter pretty well. As a biochemist, I even understood something about the complexities of DNA – genes, the simple but effective code at the heart of all biological life. But then I also understood about spirituality and about Christianity. About this man Jesus, who was begotten not made, who was God's son pointing us to the Father, who was the way, the gate through whom we all have to pass to get to eternal life.

For me this had been an exciting process, gradually learning and comprehending some of these statements of Jesus for myself. Trying then to live a life based on faith. Living a life that saw more than just the world around me but one that also pointed to something more infinite and lasting. At the time this process was characterized by developing faith from the future backwards. All faith was based on a conception of the gospel that ensured that I was going to get to heaven because I had accepted Jesus. In this scheme of things we could cope with life's difficulties in the knowledge that eternal life was secured, banked away, ready and waiting when it was all finally over.

Spirituality, then, was a purely reasoned affair. In this sense it wasn't spiritual at all. I understood this supernatural dimension to life but it didn't mean that my life in any way had a spiritual dimension to it. I had satisfied myself that in all eventualities I would experience the full measure of this spiritual life, because I had accepted Jesus, the gateway to it. I had got my ticket. Spirituality was an experience lived out in expectation of a certain kind of future.

The present was therefore all right as long as the present treated me well. Living a faith that reflected eternity backwards was fine as long as things in the present didn't seem to contradict what was being reflected. If I could get along with life conforming to the reflected image of eternity then I was happy. The problem was that it wasn't long before it didn't. It was at that point I seemed to find myself with a number of choices. I could say, well, that means that eternity isn't what you thought it was, ditch it and survive in the harsh reality of the present. Or I could say, eternity's fine just where it is and I'll just live in the present material world without thinking too much about eternity. Or you can search for meaning in the contradiction.

The latter, thankfully, conforms mostly to what happened to me after that period, and particularly through the first year of Jacob's life. It also conforms most closely to the image of Christianity C. S. Lewis creates (quoted at the beginning of the chapter). It is an image that reveals that the nature of the

Christian experience on this earth, in the present era that we find ourselves in, is one that recognizes the limitations of the created order. It acknowledges that we are indeed sculptures closer to death than to life, and that's a fact from which we cannot escape. But there is a rumour, circulating in the present of real life, of something greater and beyond. It is something we experience sufficiently to keep the rumour alive. It's an experience that contradicts the limitations of physical and biological existence, but looking from that point forwards rather than reflecting backwards. It is such a tantalizing rumour that it is worth dropping everything else and exploring in the here and now.

On the night that Jacob was born I drove home and watched a football match on television. I watched 22 grown men bash a white leather ball round a muddy pitch. Perhaps I did this because I needed to come back to earth again. I needed to remind myself that the present was physical and tangible. Looking back, what I was experiencing was the parallel nature of *bios* and *zoe*. In this parallel nature the spiritual breaks through into the physical and knocks us for six. Reasonable faith, looking forwards to life in all its fullness on the other side of the celestial gates, is challenged by that just as much as reasonable atheism that is concerned only with matter and has no room for the spiritual. I had experienced a concentrated dose of the contradicting times we live in, where matter and spirit coexist. Where we 'come in and go out' and run with wolves just like everyone else, yet with the voice of Jesus in our ear.

NOTE

1   C. S. Lewis, *Mere Christianity*, London: HarperCollins 1977.

~II~

The life we made is fading,
Colour blanching by day,
The first ruddy red-blush shade
Bled out. Like lines of hay
Piled passive in the summer heat.
To accentuate
The needles dig to meet
The tiny lanes of latent
Life lurking underneath your skin –
A drop of you for testing.

Your life is numbers now,
Imbalanced equilibrium, delicate equations,
Bad statistics, eked out at our persuasion
And going down, going down.

~2~

Decline

Naked I came from my mother's womb, and naked I shall depart.
The Lord gave and the Lord has taken away;
may the name of the Lord be praised.

Job 1.21

I cannot really ever remember a point when I questioned what was going on as Jacob became ill. This was partly because he became ill gradually and imperceptibly. It was the rather cruel opposite of the inability of parents to notice their children growing until the grandparents arrive and exclaim, 'Oh, hasn't she grown!' There are photographs of Jacob at the very worst point of his illness that I cannot bear to look at, partly because he is virtually unrecognizable as Jacob, but more because he is so clearly a very ill child and we, while acknowledging he was ill, didn't really realize how shocking he looked. It was the reaction of others that alerted and alarmed us. Somehow, however, the protective qualities of parent psychology ensured that we were sheltered from a perpetual state of anxiety at the sight of our child.

On the other hand, we did plenty of worrying and heart-searching over the course of the first three months of Jacob's life, as the situation got progressively worse. Initially our overtures of anxiety were calmed by professionals who would cast us as overconcerned first-timers. First his inability to put on weight was addressed, but thought to be not unusual; he would catch up eventually. Even while he was failing to put on hardly any weight at all we were very caringly given plenty of explanations regarding the exceptions of baby growth. Even as Jacob's growth flat-lined, there were few voices generating genuine concern. Genuine first-timers like us took these words as assurance, but then returned home to fret and worry as before.

I do not bear any resentment in reflection for this. It is the standard reaction of health professionals to reassure, and to try to encourage you as you take care of another life other than your own for the very first time. The vast majority of babies brought by their parents to doctors with worries and anxieties do indeed have absolutely nothing wrong with them. They get beyond an apparently anomalous initial phase of growth and development and carry on 'normally'. I am saying this to illustrate the very gradual and almost subversive way that genuine illness crept into our lives. Jacob's slow descent into illness and towards death duped us. It was not the sudden pain of a car crash or heart attack; it was a quiet shift from the joy of a new life, with all its hope and potential, to a situation where we couldn't quite relate to this new life of ours any more.

What we entered into was ambiguity and mystery, the unknown. Suffering in all its forms is unpleasant and un-wanted. What is perhaps most painful of all is the suffering of the unknown. There are countless stories in our newspapers and other media of people spending years of their life trying to discover the unknown facts of the death of a relative or friend. They are experiencing, far more than we, the peculiar pain of the unknown. The unknown is a situation of limbo, of suspension. We are not sure whether to hope or to grieve, we cannot confront but then nor can we ignore. The tension between life and death is with us all the time and it hurts like hell. It is a sickness that does not leave us alone and assaults our senses every minute of every day. That is the kind of tension we lived for about two months, one that intensified as time went on, as we spent more and more time in the paediatric clinic and as more and more blood was taken out of Jacob's body for testing. Jacob became extremely anaemic, until only blood transfusions on a fortnightly basis kept his haemoglobin levels up. He developed a raw and bleeding rash on his legs that refused to heal. He brought up the entire contents of his stomach sometimes as often as five or six times a day. He began to puff up as though he were obese, while putting on absolutely no weight at all. It became increasingly clear to us that the situation was no longer trivial, no longer salvageable through kind words and the passage of time. It was a situation that entertained every conceivable scenario between recovery and a full life and the worst scenario of all, death itself.

Somewhere in that agonizing tension we hung on to faith. Looking back now, this in itself seems quite remarkable. Where was the questioning? Where was the rage? Where was the inevitable cry of 'Why is this happening to me?' We went to a church that seemed to revel in family, in those who were pregnant, in the production of each new child, and in the providence of children. And here we were, finally, after several years of watching other people's happy, healthy and 'normal' kids scurrying around us, with our first child, destined surely, like them, to be 'normal', struggling to imagine if he might ever walk, talk or even live at all. And yet the standard questions didn't come.

As it proved, they came later. In the meantime something sustained us. We had a relationship with God that suddenly came into focus as never before. All that Emily and I had staked our lives on abruptly mattered. And our faith held: shaken, but it held. Jesus told a story of two men who built houses, one on sand and the other on rock. In both storms come but only in one does the house remain standing. Jesus completes the story by saying that he is that rock. My goodness, did that story suddenly make sense in a new way.

I wonder, however, whether it would have done had it not been for periods of demolition and rebuilding of my own faith after I left university. At that time I had what I considered to be pretty solid faith. I had left school a Christian but was completely ignorant of even the most rudimentary understanding of the gospel. I graduated three years later with a degree in biochemistry and what amounted to another in evangelical theology. The latter equipped me with a multi-dimensional and almost exhaustive grounding in the work of Christ on the cross. The gospel was about redemption, substitution, vicarious suffering, propitiation and umpteen other academic terms that served to deepen our understanding of exactly what was going on when Jesus was crucified. Christianity was about deepening and affirming these beliefs, and the material that supported them in the various books of the Bible. It was also about bringing others into that superior understanding. The Bible was a text to be studied meticulously, verse by verse if possible, even better with others, and one on one at its absolute zenith.

It was all fantastic stuff. In an academic environment it was perfect. Everyone had questions and we had answers. Apologetics was king. Converts were won through having the right answers to the standard refutations of Christianity. The answers were all there; you simply had to know them.

After leaving university answers were suddenly harder to come by. I spent a year teaching in a remote part of Kenya and another working for a parish church in the east end of Glasgow. In both these environments I encountered questions for which I had few answers. These were real-life questions, not academic ones. They were tangible questions, not thought experiments. They were about me and people and things that really mattered, not about the Bible or the cross, or the origin of evil, or the reality of hell or the person of Jesus. They were questions that germinated from the inconsistencies between an academically rigorous faith and a deeply ambiguous world, from the certainties of evangelical theology and the inherent mysteries of me and the world I inhabited.

Why were my prayers going unanswered? Why did disadvantaged people on the housing estate where I lived and worked, in need of hope and salvation as blatantly and immediately as any group of people I had ever met, seem to have a wholesale aversion to the claims of Christianity and of Christ? Why did this part of the world seem to get endlessly worse instead of better? Why did 'successful' churches thrive in affluent areas and not poor areas? Why did this church with a vibrant and tenacious group of faithful people struggle year after year? Why did people come so far with their faith and then let go? More personally, why couldn't I seem to change myself into who I wanted to be? Why did I always come up against the same unscalable walls that I had neither the wisdom nor the strength to climb over?

My faith collapsed like a house of cards. I lost all sense of what faith was supposed to be about and why I had entertained it in the first place. I lost any passion for Christianity. In particular I had grown tired of a theology of right and wrong – a theology that seemed to think it had all the answers but seemed to me to need above all to ask questions. In my worst moments I lost my fundamental belief in God. After all, if God couldn't turn his hand to help me, and if this great successful gospel that had all the answers had no impact in the place where it was really needed, then I guessed that perhaps God was after all not God at all.

Eventually I went to see somebody who gave me the best advice of my life. He suggested that I stop going to church and stop reading the Bible. He advised me not to pray and not to think about Christianity one little bit. I left this wise man that evening as though somebody had finally shown me the way out of a maze. The cramped and claustrophobic environment I had been in suddenly fell away behind me and a new horizon of infinite possibilities opened up. This man had given me the best present I had ever had, the freedom to do nothing. I had been doing things at the insistence of others for so long; finally I met somebody who told me to do nothing.

This was the beginning of a journey home, a long process of rebuilding on the foundation not of bookish, academic, workaholic Christianity but gentle, organic, light-burden-easy-yoke relationship-based Christianity. A Christianity that had less mind and more heart and soul – one that had room for failure, room for doubt and room for the unknown. Little did I know that very gently, by an infinitely loving and compassionate God, I had been prepared for the future.

Innocent suffering or a malicious God?

It was five years between leaving university and having Jacob. Five years in which I had done four jobs, lived in three countries and got married. Five years in which I had, slowly and at times painfully, been taught a crucial lesson by God. It is the same lesson that God, rather more dramatically, teaches Job. Job, after hearing God barrage him with endless questions about the whole of creation, from the depths of the earth to the far reaches of the universe, none of which he can even begin to answer (and few of which can we, even with our superior knowledge), makes the utterly humble and faithful statement: 'Surely I spoke of things I did not understand, things too wonderful for me to know' (Job 42.3).

So when Jacob's descent into illness became real, the question 'Why is this happening to me?' *did* surface, but in the context of a relationship with God that gave space for unknowing. On the other hand I was human. In more sober moments I quietly wondered what I had done to deserve what was happening. I echoed the ambient attitude of the modern world, which essentially believes we get what we deserve. And perhaps it echoed more sonorously for me, because it was not the first time in our family that something malevolent with a genetic origin had struck. When I was 21 we lost Jill, my sister. She had a rather cruel and meaningless genetic condition called MPS. This expresses itself in a gradual deterioration of everything, beginning with the brain, making slow and inexorable progress over the whole of a sufferer's life, until there is nothing much left. My sister spent the final years of her life in a wheelchair, unable to do anything by herself, completely dependent on carers. Towards the end she was probably unaware of anybody she might once have conceived of as friend or family.

As her younger brother I had a rather strange perspective on Jill's illness. To me she was always ill, always different; she went to special schools and inhabited a very different world from me. I never really questioned why this had happened to our family and why Jill had been affected by this horrible condition. When Jacob became ill it was actually my mother who forced me to ask why. Why was this happening to us? My mother came to stay with us in the midst of the critical phase of Jacob's illness and diagnosis. Her reaction was perfectly understandable. Why should two such cruel injustices happen so close to each other in the same family? It was a question that had to be answered. After all, statistically speaking the chances of two children in successive generations being hit by such rare genetic disorders was literally millions to one. In a nation of lotteries and scratch cards, where we fascinate over the statistics of winning and losing when money is at stake, the experience of being one of the losers in life's lottery of suffering is ironic and cruel. It is diametrically opposed to the 'It could be you!' upbeat mentality of the lottery's marketing spin-doctors. Yes, it really could be you. You never thought it really could. After all, it always 'happens to other people'. Suddenly it's happening to you. Suddenly it was happening to us, and inevitably, almost innately, we asked why.

One explanation that surfaces is that it's because of you. Statistical improbabilities can be explained away if there is a cause for it all; if somewhere in the past, even distant past, a hidden sin lies lurking, for which this is the payment. This response to suffering may make little sense. It may be a cruel explanation but it is deeply satisfying for many for the precise reason that it gives us an answer – a fairly unpleasant one, but nevertheless an answer. It enables us to conceive of a world that makes sense and one that is fairly simple. If you're good, good things happen to you; if you're bad, bad things happen to you. Simple, effective and just.

Theologically speaking, this world-view suggests that sin equates with suffering and, the reverse, good equates with happiness. Apparently unjust suffering and pain are therefore inconsistent with this, and the natural conclusion is either to cast oneself as unknowingly sinful or to see God as a liar and a crook. Not only that, a faith in God built on this supposition logically means that we really only believe in God because our faith will result in a pain-free and happy existence, protected from the realities and randomness of the world.

This is exactly the premise that the book of Job is built on. It will come as no surprise that the book of Job became a well-thumbed area of the Bible during this time. Suddenly this long, difficult and somewhat obtuse book came sharply into focus, as the story of a man who suffered unjustly began to cross-cut with our own developing story of suffering. For the book of Job starts with a wager between God and Satan on the very notion, proposed by Satan, that Job actually only loves God because he's comfortable, because Job equates his fortunate position with God's favour. 'Does Job fear God for nothing?' says the Devil. 'Stretch out your hand and strike everything he has, and he will surely curse you to your face' (Job 1.9, 11).

Satan bets with God that Job's legendary faith and laudable behaviour will wilt and perish to nothing. More than that, Job will actually turn to hating God, because Job's faith is based on what he gets out of it. If what he gets out of it suddenly disappears then what will be left will be little or nothing at all. This is the wager.

The thing is, neither Job nor his friends who come to comfort him in the aftermath of his calamities know anything about this wager. They are completely ignorant of the origin of this terrible series of disasters that happen upon Job. They are left to sit in the dust, the ashes and other remnants of Job's life simply to speculate and theorize what that origin might be. They are in the unknown, where there are no easy answers but where easy answers have a bad and dangerous habit of being proposed.

So it is that they begin to address Job, who in a rapid catalogue of numbing catastrophe has lost everything: possessions, family, livelihood and status. One by one Job's friends insist that there must surely be some underground area of sinfulness in him that has caused his terrible suffering. After countless speeches by Job where he protests his innocence to his friends, one of them finally blurts, 'What man is like Job, who drinks scorn like water? He keeps company with evildoers; he associates with wicked men ... To his sin he adds rebellion' (Job 34.7, 8, 37).

It is simply incomprehensible to them that Job could have suffered in the way that he had for no reason, and as the reason cannot lie with God then it must lie with Job. Yet the writer of Job has gone to great trouble to tell us that Job is innocent. Three times in the first two chapters of the book we are told that Job is 'blameless and upright', that he 'fears God and shuns evil' (Job 1.1, 8; 2.3). For many the book of Job sits uncomfortably in the Bible, to show us that yes indeed, shit happens. Further than that, it happens to those of us who believe in the Christian God just as much as those who don't. There *is* such as thing as innocent suffering. And while this appears to challenge all our selfish and sometimes innate notions of how the world should work, this is the stark reality of the world in its present broken order.

Therefore in the face of suffering that defied odds and any rational explanation, the book of Job gave me an anchor of sorts. It said that the just suffer unjustly. I was not alone. I had not been somehow specially chosen, in the manner of a mail-order firm or a *Reader's Digest* promotion. But then nor had I brought it upon myself. No doubt there were hidden sins in my life but chastising myself towards destruction in a bid to find them, confess them and somehow purge them out was not going to be of any use to anyone. Nor was it likely to miraculously bring back our child from the brink. What Job taught me was that there was no quid pro quo with God. God was not up there looking for reasons to bring suffering upon me or to bring down retributive justice on his people. We like to think that he would but that's not the God of the book of Job.

There is, of course, another response to the issue of unjust suffering. While the cause of what was happening may not have rested on us, it may after all rest with God himself. Perhaps this God whom we had thought of as loving was not like this at all. Perhaps our notion of a loving and benevolent God was utterly and tragically wrong. Had we been duped naively into believing that there really was an ultimately good force at work in the universe?

We live in an intensely cynical age, one that somehow would rather not believe in love, ultimate love, love that is really loving. We would rather have a love that serves itself than one that genuinely serves others. This is partly the result of a breakdown in our own sense of solidarity with one another. If we ourselves cannot achieve genuine love, if we strive but continue to fail to love purely out of selfless motives, purely because those we love are innately worth loving, then we conclude that that is because love doesn't exist. Further, we would prefer to see around us evidence that it doesn't exist – that there is no source of selfless love in the universe. We would rather live in a satisfactory world than one where something greater than satisfactory is out there but beyond our grasp.

This is well illustrated by the media frenzy at the breaking up of glamour couples. As I write the media is full of stories of the separation of one of Hollywood's longest surviving married couples, Nicole Kidman and Tom Cruise. On the surface there seems to be a great deal of mourning at the end of their relationship. On the other hand, in their glamour, talent and apparent odds-defying ability to love each other in the context of Hollywood and stardom, the sheer glee with which we gorge on the tale of their demise as a couple seems to suggest that we are rather relieved. We are relieved to find evidence that genuine love, that overcomes all that is thrown at it, might prove to be unreliable. We can therefore once again return to the banality and scant satisfaction of our own lives, safe in the understanding that this is after all as good as it gets.

Those then who hold a belief in a genuinely loving God do so in the context of a cynical age that is virtually predisposed to believing the opposite in order to maintain the status quo. Suffering, unjust suffering in particular, provides a stern challenge for such believers. For when suffering comes, the believer has to hold on in an arena where the whispers of 'I told you so' begin to grow in volume all around.

When C. S. Lewis's wife died, he wrote down his thoughts. They were first published anonymously, but are now with us as *A Grief Observed*. It is an intensely frank series of reflections on grief, affording the reader the unsettling privilege of journeying with C. S. Lewis through the turmoil of his feelings, thoughts and faith in the days and weeks after his bereavement. At the beginning, he states that perhaps his greatest danger is not that his grief might make him less likely to believe in God but that it might reveal a God he doesn't like very much: 'What room have we, except our own desperate wishes, to believe that God is, by any standard we conceive, "good"? Doesn't all the prima facie evidence suggest exactly the opposite?'[1]

Lewis felt like a man who had been seductively enticed up the garden path only to find that something hideous and malicious lay in wait for him. What greeted him was not the loving visage he had been led to expect but something sinister and frightening.

The rock of relationship

Such thoughts and doubts were there for us as Jacob slipped ever further from health and from our world. Eventually there was anger – strong, almost aggressive emotion towards God that shocked us both. Yet on reflection it seems that two things were going on, at different levels. On the surface we agonized, doubted and expressed anger, but at other times we were faithful and trusting. A whole spectrum of belief and unbelief seemed to be visible at the surface during that period. However, we were not swung in our doubts about God so much that any attachment to him was broken. What tethered us to God, thankfully, was something deeper and stronger. It was a relationship that continued to persuade us that while some of our questions went unanswered we had enough knowledge and experience of God to keep going and to hang on. We were not prevented from asking some pretty fundamental questions, but we found that our faith was not allowed to hinge on those questions alone. In effect this freed us up to concentrate on some of the practical issues at hand, the sort of day-to-day business of hospitals, tests, conversations with medical staff and so on that take up so much time and energy. We were freed to concentrate our energies on those things, leaving the unanswered questions in the hands of God.

It was as if we were out at sea in a prolonged storm. Anyone who has sailed a boat knows what a complicated exercise this is and in the midst of a storm you need all your energies, mental and physical, to ensure that the boat is maintained upright and not swallowed by the waves. At such a time there is little time for questioning. You do not go below decks to look at the weather charts of previous weeks to examine what meteorological forces brewed such a fierce storm. Rather, every moment is spent on deck ensuring that everything is done to try to give you the best possible chance of getting through the storm in one piece. Once the storm has passed and calmer waters return, you may well sit with others who have experienced the same storm, compare notes, wonder how you could have coped better and discuss the origins of the storm itself. That is the safe and sensible time to do it.

This was very much our experience. As the storm raged we hunkered down, did what was necessary to get through, cried out to God and left many unanswered questions with him. Our relationship with God had enough space for unknowing that what might have become a crisis of faith did not do so. A time that raised deep questions about faith and the place of suffering did not also become the time that required these questions to be answered.

Strangely enough, though, this concept of a relationship with God would very often seem to be based on knowing rather than unknowing. In order to have a meaningful relationship with God we have to get to know him. Frequently this process of knowing God can be very academic, almost scientific. We can get to know God in the same way that we might get to know the three-dimensional structure of DNA or the chemical composition of our own tears, by dividing them up into their constituent parts and putting them back together.

My father tells a story of having to instruct his men how to use a newly introduced gun at the beginning of the Second World War. He knew no more about this new gun than the men he commanded. So he spent all night taking this gun to pieces, examining every part and putting it back together again. He now knew about the gun sufficiently to teach his men the next day. But did he know what it felt like to hold that gun on the battlefield? Did he know its idiosyncrasies? Its susceptibility to jamming? Its durability? Its state and performance after weeks and months of use in the open air, the wet and the mud? Did he know its character, the sort of character that reveals itself only with use and the test of time and circumstances?

That is nevertheless how we often think we can 'know' God, by pulling him to pieces and putting him back together again. Then we tell others that this is indeed God and we know him. We also feel that if there is something we feel we don't know about God then it only requires an extra module or course that somehow we missed out on earlier to fill the gap in our knowledge.

What we discovered, on reflection, as all that seemed tangible and knowable ebbed away in front of us, was that in order to really know we have to admit that there's so much that we don't know. We have to let go at some point of that idiotic notion that God is thoroughly knowable – that he can be defined to the nth degree or categorized and theorized to suit every ramification that life throws at us. At some point we have to just let go and say that God is God. Within that confession of faith lies the scope and possibility of unknowing.

Once again, Job comes out the victor in this regard. Buffeted from all directions by his friends, who thought they were genuinely helping him through his troubles, he makes the journey from submission to submission. He travels from a state where he confesses his implicit faith in God, no matter what, to a state where he confesses it again, though perhaps with an even greater sense of why he was right to have this implicit faith at all.

Job's first reaction to his suffering, with the words of the final messenger still reverberating incredulously in his ears, is to utter a statement of completely irrational faith: 'Naked I come from my mother's womb, and naked I shall depart. The Lord gave and the Lord has taken away; may the name of the Lord be praised' (Job 1.21). And while this statement comes in for severe testing throughout the rest of the book, this is where Job starts his journey. He knows God and he knows that there is something infinitely unknowable about him.

At the end of his odyssey of faith and doubt he returns to a similar state. God has spoken. Job has roused him and pestered him enough to elicit a response, a wild and almost apocalyptic discourse on unknowing that takes Job from the depths of the ocean to the ends of the universe. Job is shown God's museum – not of the things that are known to man, like the vast and impressive exhibits of the Natural History Museum that boast of all that we know, but of the things that we do not. God's speech suggests that if we were to attempt to house such a museum of unknowing we would require a rather larger building.

And at the end of this great exhibition Job is sufficiently awed. In the visitors' book he writes his testimony to unknowing: 'Surely I spoke of things I did not understand, things too wonderful for me to know' (Job 42.3). He has let go and admitted what we try so hard to avoid admitting, that there is more to this than we can ever know. We are not gods, all knowing and if not knowing then capable of knowing. There is a limit to our knowing which is probably well short of all there is to know and paradoxically, in line with many of the ways God seems to act, in letting go of our cult of knowledge we truly begin to know God.

So it was that as our world began to be filled more and more with the atmosphere and vocabulary of suffering I simply had to echo Job's statement at the beginning of his own wrestle with God, that while we would question and explore as much as we and our broken world enabled us, God was God

– 'The Lord gave and the Lord has taken away; may the name of the Lord be praised.'

NOTE

1   C. S. Lewis, *A Grief Observed*, London: Faber and Faber 1961.

~III~

An odd place to let the anger run,
Through the steep, wood-chipped paths
Of Crarae's retrieved gardens.
Briars amidst rhododendrons
Like a diseased laugh
Into which the humour hardens.

You won't remember the nervous presence
Of a red squirrel, twitch-tense,
Small-seeming, with a rust-washed colour
The imbibed aggression of its brother.

A vestige of a species,
Like an obstinate pulse under the skin
Over which the force of a thousand diseases,
Virulent and unspecified, cannot win.

~3~

Nadir

After this, Job opened his mouth and cursed the day of his birth.
Job 3.1

Every act of rebellion conceals an unconscious aspiration towards acceptance, and every act of acceptance is still hot with the rebellion that gave rise to it.

Paul Tournier[1]

It is strange how without feeling you can be in the midst of impending or present tragedy. This was perhaps particularly true for me – supporting a wife whose first attempt at motherhood was falling apart before her eyes, I remained reasonably stoic in the days and weeks during which Jacob got progressively worse. All the processing in my head had a strange idealism that, looking back on it, now seems ridiculous.

I spent much time talking to a colleague who had lost his wife to cancer. He too had learnt to be circumspect about his experience; he was now beyond it and well into forging a new life out of what was left of the old. I found myself talking to him as one who had experienced as he had, had learnt what he had learnt. There was even a taste of condescension about the way I spoke to him. Clear-thinking me had worked through the experience of suffering even while it arrested my senses every day.

But that is how it was. There was so little distance between suffering – the sight of Jacob getting worse, with no evidence of any explanation on the horizon – and the rest of life that carried on as normal. Jacob's descent was fast becoming a thought experiment rather than an experience. I was so taken up by the cerebral wrestling that was going on inside of me that I was forgetting how to feel about what was going on.

There was always the suspicion, however, that feeling would catch up with me. Surely I could not forever rationalize my feeling into submission? Surely my ability to contain what I was experiencing within the bounds of my neat and tidy world-view would not last forever? Surely at some point the plain reality of the injustice of what was happening was going to hit me between the eyes? And what then? What would come out? What happens when you no longer have words? When all your explanations and pious rationalizations come to an end, and a cliff that you are compelled to go beyond finally lies at your feet?

There is inevitably a point when this happens in an experience of suffering. Such a precipice may also present itself for no apparent reason or as a result of an accumulation of apparently small and manageable trials. It happens to so many people: they can go no further on the premises and assumptions upon which they have travelled safely so far. The limits of faith, stoicism, pride, obstinacy, theology, or whatever else we dogmatically confine ourselves with, are finally reached and we are forced to go beyond, or return.

Towards the edge
After about a month of increasingly frequent visits to the hospital with a boy who wasn't getting any better, we finally reached our first day of reckoning. It had been a frustrating and arduous journey for us so far. We had placed our baby into the hands of innumerable GPs, registrars, junior doctors and consultants and nothing any of them did seemed to improve our son's health. At times, it must be said, we wondered whether Jacob had become something of an interesting case for our particular consultant. His symptoms were rare and confusing. He was like a novel little riddle that consumed the hungry mind of the medical profession for a time. We increasingly got the feeling that this was one

particular riddle our consultant wanted to keep for himself. It was one that he had his particular way of solving. He was a haematologist and Jacob had particularly interesting haematological symptoms. His was therefore a riddle that was to be solved haematologically.

At the same time, however, Jacob was digestively deranged. He kept precious little food down, vomiting it out in great gushes, and continued to fail to put anything but an ounce or two of weight on. We were increasingly convinced that there were two ways to solve this riddle, and the present approach was using only one of them.

At no point were we given the opportunity ourselves to help solve the riddle. While we could provide the elements of the equation – the number of times he was being sick, his behaviour, the colour of his nappies and other details – we were left out of the laboratory when it came to trying to make sense of all these. It seemed increasingly that Jacob was a baby being reduced to statistics, the numbers that detailed his critical functions. What defined Jacob, to those who were attempting to cure him, were his weight and his haemoglobin levels. On those two statistics Jacob's future appeared to rest.

With each trip to the hospital we thought we were edging ever closer to some sort of climax. What defined that climax could be anything from cure to incurable, from hope to hopelessness, from life to death. Each day contained all the infinite possibilities contained within that vast scope. We held on to the glimmer of hope every time his blood haemoglobin level held, or when he put on a tiny amount of weight, or each time the doctor told stories of freak viruses that caused all manner of symptoms, all infinitely curable. And yet we also entertained the nightmare scenarios of rare terminal illnesses with a slow and painful trajectory inexorably aimed at death.

However, at least in that last state there is the possibility of healing and restoration. The Christian faith would seem to accommodate insane and illogical hope – the hope beyond all hope that fills so many stories of Jesus' ministry: blind Bartimaeus healed after a lifetime of blindness, the woman healed after years of internal bleeding. There is also the hope beyond all possible hope of Lazarus, and of Jairus' daughter, hope that defies natural science and crosses our assumed limits and suppositions about where life ends and death begins. To be frank, though, such hope was there in our faith only as long as the medical profession held out their version of hope to us. God could use the NHS to heal Jacob, but would he if the NHS failed? Therefore we prayed for the grace of God through the medical profession to bring our own little Lazarus back to life. While not doubting that God could intervene and make all things well we did doubt that he would. Faith in Jacob's healing rested heavily on the ability of the medical staff working with us to crack the riddle, apply the medicine and send us home with a recovering child.

That is, until finally we were cut loose. That day we went into the hospital, as on numerous previous occasions, hopeful and full of dread at the same time. Each time Jacob's blood was taken was a trial, not just actually getting the blood out of him, but also getting enough. Then there was the dilemma of which tests to do on which samples. Each time we visited the clinic we would receive the results of these tests, most of which were inconclusive.

I now know how to tell when medics have reached a conclusion. Or rather, I can recognize when they have reached a bad and unwanted conclusion. We were sitting in the clinic, among the usual mêlée of other children of various ages and severities of illness. This was the strange public/private space where the television blared out daytime chat while a nurse examined Jacob or left him attached to a drip. Curtains being pulled around you gave the suggestion of privacy while you were inside them and a kind of nervous empathy to those outside. Our experience of the hospital was of this space, or of the treatment room where Jacob was subjected to the fumblings of registrars and SHOs with needles, hunting for lost veins. Meanwhile outside one of us would cringe or cry at the sound of his screaming.

Today was different. Our congenial and pleasant consultant beckoned us to another room and we were joined by a nurse and a registrar. While the consultant sat at his desk, facing us, the nurse sat some way away, disengaged but present. We kind of knew that this was bad and we were about to be told so. Our consultant spent some ten minutes agonizing with us over the results of the latest set of tests. He was moving towards something but going through the processes of information that were required. He said he thought he knew what the problem was but he needed to be sure. How sure was he? Ninety-five per cent. Was that not sure enough? He would rather be 100 per cent. Well, we were happy with 95 per cent if he was. OK.

That day, Jacob was diagnosed with a rare genetic condition known as Pearson's syndrome. While we sat in stunned attention the consultant described to us that this meant that Jacob's cells were not capable of making enough energy to carry out their essential functions. This particularly affected cells that divided rapidly, such as blood cells, stomach cells and skin cells. This neatly explained why Jacob was chronically anaemic, failed to put on any weight and why he had a raw rash all the way down his legs that refused to heal. The riddle had been solved.

I knew enough about genetics to understand this explanation. It meant that Jacob would be unable to fight infection properly; even the feeblest infection would be a challenge to him. It meant that he would need continuous blood transfusions to give him a normal level of blood cells. It meant that he would struggle to walk properly because his muscles wouldn't be strong enough, he would wobble at best. It meant almost certainly that he would live a life of the lowest quality and scantest expectancy. It really was our worst-case scenario.

At the edge

When something like this happens it is as if you have been hit by a train. Initially you feel the most extreme pain. We cried the most intense tears in that small room after the consultant had left – intense but short-lived. After that there is shock and a kind of delirium as you try to grapple with the monstrous thing that you hoped you would never have to face. In our case the shock and delirium seemed to express itself in a gracious attempt to make everything all right. Not in the sense of saying that nothing mattered – that this wasn't really happening – but in the sense of reasoning ourselves into a way of thinking that made everything bearable.

Within half an hour of receiving the news we were sitting having tea in the hospital, beginning to construct life again. We began to build a serious and well thought-out structure of common sense that, while not making light of what happened, made possible a brave and capable response. The next day I spoke to our vicar. I told him the news as though I were reading it from a script. I told him how we were going to cope. I even ventured to tell him why this was happening, why God had allowed this, and that perhaps in some way there was some rational timing about it all.

None of what I said may have been wrong; it all made sense. For example, I told myself and others that you had to be careful in defining what normality was. What did it mean when we said to people that during pregnancy we prayed and hoped simply that our child was normal? What did it mean when we said that all we hoped for was that our child would have a normal life? Spending so much time in a paediatric clinic had given me a different perspective on normality. Normality in that particular environment was sickness, often serious sickness. This was the normality of things going wrong, the normality of early parenthood nightmares coming true and the platitudes and reassurance of midwives and health visitors proving to be meaningless. The house where my sister had lived had been filled with children with the most serious degenerative conditions. It was normal there for children to be incapable of looking after themselves, for them to spend all day in a chair or wheelchair, burbling incoherently or crying inconsolably for hours. It was also normal for them to die young and for their parents and those of the other children to gather to say goodbye and to celebrate their life like any other family mourning a lost one. What we were dealing with then was normality – the sharp end of it perhaps, but normality none the less. The world is a fallen place and to respond to these things as if they didn't happen, as if they were abnormal, is not consistent with the state of the world.

To some extent I still think in this way, although it is a time-limited view. But I wonder how on earth I managed to think this on that day, with the knowledge of my son's illness only 24 hours old. I imagine there are many more people who courageously and resolutely manage through their pain with such reasonableness. It is a rationality that makes sense; it is helpful and supportive but surely lacks something passionate; something that taps the sheer awfulness of suffering and expresses the fact that this isn't the way it was meant to be, and that the way it presently is is blatantly horrific. In retrospect, while shock and delirium played their part, I wonder whether, on that day and in the days afterwards, we were exploring the edge. Reason had taken me to the edge but something quite different was going to take me further. I have enormous respect for those who can hold on to reason in the face of enduring pain. However, for me there was somewhere beyond reason and bravery, something that required me to jump off the cliff at my feet and hope that something caught me. For us that thing was anger, an anger that welled up within us almost unawares, an anger that overtook us and pulled us in its wake over the cliff and into the abyss.

The anger runs
We were walking in the gardens of an old house on the west coast of Scotland a few days after Jacob's diagnosis. The consultant had suggested we take a week's holiday to come to terms with the situation and to prepare ourselves for the long haul ahead. We would then return to London and Jacob would go into hospital for a stay in order to treat his symptoms and get him on some kind of even keel. We were quiet that day, even jovial, enjoying the gardens and not

talking much. Then I can remember saying that I wasn't happy any more accepting the way things were, not asking the question 'Why is this happening to us?' Suddenly that question 'Why is this happening to us?' became essential – it had to be asked! It was an experience that brought me to my senses. For goodness sake, of course it isn't unheard of for people to suffer in the way we were, but this was happening to *us* and it was intensely painful. Somehow in my neat reasonableness I had depersonalized the whole situation. While suffering has a universal quality, that doesn't make the particular any less painful. Right now we were in the particular and it hurt like hell.

That day an anger ran from me towards God in a way that would have seemed blasphemous earlier in my Christian life. It burst from me in language and feelings towards God that were intense and irreverent. I uttered language to God that seemed to bypass the usual semantic filters we use when praying – it was rough, raw and above all real. This was my soul talking instead of my sensible self.

This burst of anger affected us profoundly. I had never found myself to be angry with God in the way that I was that day. I had never uttered such words before in that way, with real venom and real anguish, words that came not from the thinking part of me but straight from the feeling part of me. It was a surprising sensation but it also made me nervous, for suddenly I was exploring areas I had never been in before. It was also dangerous, because part of me thought that perhaps this was blasphemy and renunciation. I automatically felt almost ashamed at this outburst. I could sense the disapproval of a church whose evangelical culture finds little space for honest emotions, that illuminate the negative aspects of our experience as the people of God on this earth. Surely this wasn't progression but regression; I had finally rebelled like a teenager who can't take it any more. Would I not therefore find myself punished for such an outburst? How could I speak with God like this and expect to get away with it?

It was in exploring the experience and reaction of Job, then and later on, however, that helped me discover the value of anger in our Christian lives. Even a cursory reading of Job begins to reveal the place of anger in the geography of faith. For while Job's reaction to his first set of trials is hugely humble and worshipful, the reaction to the second is pure vitriol:

After this, Job opened his mouth and cursed the day of his birth. He said:
  'May the day of my birth perish,
   and the night it was said "A boy is born!"
  That day – may it turn to darkness;
   may God above not care about it;
   may no light shine upon it.' (Job 3.1–4)

Later he specifically accuses God of wronging him and openly challenges God's character, implying that God is silent, unjust and hostile:

  Then know that God has wronged me and drawn
  his net around me.
  Though I cry, 'I've been wronged!' I get no response;
  though I call for help, there is no justice.
  He has blocked my way so that I cannot pass;
  he has shrouded my paths in darkness.
  He has stripped me of my honour
  and removed the crown from my head.
  He tears me down on every side till I am gone;
  he uproots my hope like a tree.
  His anger burns against me... (Job 19.6–11)

Meanwhile his three friends keep their heads. They give great long speeches of rationality that never venture to call God into question, only Job. Which of these would seem the most faithful, the most godly response? We get an answer to this question from God himself:

> After the Lord had said these things to Job, he said to
> Eliphaz the Temanite, 'I am angry with you and your
> two friends, because you have not spoken of me what
> is right, as my servant Job has.' (Job 42.7)

Now that must have come as something of a surprise. There's
Job shouting and screaming at God, calling his character into
question, talking directly to him, while his friends argue for
what appears to be God's case, the preservation of the justness
and goodness of God. And God says, 'You have not spoken *of
me* what is right.' They must have thought, 'We never said
anything about you, it was Job our talk was directed at.'
Meanwhile Job has spoken of God 'what is right'!

This must have been a shock to the ears of Job's friends.
Despite the existence of Job in our Bibles for centuries, it
appears to come as something of a shock to us. We seem to
have a tendency to remove the vocabulary of anger from our
language of faith. We unspokenly have a faith that associates
anger with a lack of faith and a backsliding towards atheism.
Someone expressing anger is viewed with concern at best and
derision at worst. None of us is immune – for the absence of
the expression of anger becomes part of our culture, part of
the way we do things. How would most of us react to a public
prayer of anger, or a song that expressed anger towards God?
How would we view someone who spoke openly not of their
undying love and praise for God but of their anger towards
him? I can think of precious few, if any, songs that we sing in
our own church that dare to express anger towards God. Our
passion is reduced to a staple diet of sweetness, as if everything
is all right. Perhaps expressing anger in our worship would
remind us too much of the fact that all is not perfect. Yet the
Psalms, the Hebrews' public and private worship song-book,
is littered with anger towards God, anger at his failure to hear
the cries of his people, anger at the way the unrighteous always
seem to prosper, anger at injustice and pain, and anger, like
that of Job, at innocent suffering that just doesn't seem to
make sense.

And God says of Job's anger that he has said 'what is right'! What does that mean? Does it actually mean that Job was right when he called the very character of God into question? Is God agreeing with Job about his character assessment?

Surely this is not a statement about the rights and wrongs of the words uttered by Job compared with those uttered by his friends. After all, when it comes to doctrine his friends toe a fairly sensible line, always upholding that God is good. Why is God therefore so hard on them, and favourable to Job?

Perhaps God's assessment of what has been said is not so much *what* was said but the *attitude* with which it was said. He is angry with Eliphaz and his two friends because their attitude was pious and accusatory. After a brief phase of compassion and silence, they have done little else but add to Job's woes by pontificating to him as though he knows nothing of God. Worse still, they finally succumb to the temptation to accuse him directly of wrongdoing. While the scientific examination of Job's words, written two-dimensionally in pen and ink, might leave Job looking worse off in God's eyes, he has, according to God, done what is right. He has never forsaken God. He has never taken out his anger on others. He has wrestled with all that has happened to him in a real and transparent way. He has not hidden from God the things of his heart. He has not been economical with his feelings or his thoughts. He has said it how it is. The words are raw and harsh but God has seen beyond mere words to the heart, to the source of the passion in Job for his God. Job's anger is the very expression of his love for God in the context of his suffering. Job knows and loves his God. Satan was wrong – his relationship with God was not dependent on the material stuff of life, in which he was well blessed. No, there was something deeper and more profound about Job's love of God. And God sees it where Job's friends do not, written through his hard, raw anger, like writing that appears through a stick of rock.

This is amply illustrated by another story, this time from the New Testament. The account in John's Gospel (11.1–44) of the death of Lazarus is a beautiful story of emotion and pathos that exemplifies the realities of humankind's experience of pain and God's empathy with us. Lazarus, a friend of Jesus, has become sick. Jesus, hearing of this, does not rush to heal him but delays his return to their home by some three days. By the time he gets there Lazarus is dead and his sisters, Mary and Martha, are in mourning. In turn each sister meets Jesus alone and makes the same assessment: 'Lord,' each of them says, 'if you had been here, my brother would not have died.'

It is always a risky business imposing on such words the emotion with which they were said, the tone of voice, the volume or the attitude that accompanied them. Ultimately we do not know this third dimension to the text we have inherited. However, with Mary and Martha perhaps we know enough about them to hazard a guess. For we know that Mary seemed the more intuitive, more in touch with her feelings, more open to the public expression of emotion. It was she who had earlier sat at Jesus' feet listening attentively to what he had to say. It was Mary who later anointed Jesus with hugely expensive perfume. On the other hand, Martha seems harder, more prone to anger, expending her energies more practically, busying her hands with work, putting her mind to the things that need doing. It was she who resented her sister's worship and quietness before Jesus and she serves while Mary anoints Jesus with perfume.

For these reasons, Martha's words seem to me to come out angry, Mary's passionate. Martha's come mixed with spittle while Mary's come mixed with tears. Martha's words come hot with angry passion and rueful assurance – after all, it stands to reason that if Jesus had come sooner everything would have been all right. Mary's words, on the other hand, are bruised and broken; they express a kind of humble confusion. She cannot equate what is happening with the Jesus she knows and it breaks her heart.

Whether that was the case or not is immaterial in a sense, for Jesus is able to see beyond mere words, beyond the outward visible expressions in each of them to the depths of their hearts and souls. Each of them has wrestled with their love for this divine man who has apparently let them down. Jesus, with his eyes on their hearts, does not chastise them. If Martha in particular is angry at Jesus, he is not angry with her. His response is not to banish her for her outburst but to draw her in with one of the most extraordinary revelations of his identity: 'I am the resurrection and the life'! Similarly with Mary he responds with compassion, shedding tears of his own, giving us an unbelievably vulnerable picture of our God weeping at the ghastliness of our predicament, caught in the jaws of death and powerless to do anything about it.

The purity of Mary's and Martha's emotions are in a sense rewarded by Jesus. Their willingness to put their emotions humbly and openly before God elicits a response of great power and profundity. Job's anger, his willingness to be real with God, also rouses God to speak, to reveal, to allow more of himself to be known to us. There is something about our willingness to dispense with our heads for a while in our relationship with God and lead with our heart that brings a compassionate response from God. Whether this shows itself in anger, tears, laughter or pain seems immaterial. What is important is our willingness to be honest before him.

This was certainly how it felt for us. The anger ran and we directed it at God. That first brief but significant outburst proved to be a turning-point, not necessarily in our struggles on a rational level with the injustice of what was happening, but on a relational level with God. Something in the fact that our anger did not result in the expected lightning bolt or other such retribution gave us faith and confidence. Our rash, blind anger was like a nervous shout into a darkened cave. When an enraged bear did not emerge we began to explore the darkness with greater confidence. Confidence in the possibility that beyond what we could see or could explain was not some grisly spectacle of a God waiting to consume us when we put a foot out of line, but a God who knew all about darkness and death, for after all he had been there too.

It is hard even now to put words to our experience beyond that day. In one way we were no different on the surface. We continued to ask questions. We continued to struggle with the fact that when we prayed for our son to get better, for him to make that next crucial step towards getting well again, our prayers were frequently not answered. We continued to wrestle with the dissonance between what we thought we knew about God and our daily experience. What took place was perhaps something of a paradigm shift. A change in perspective that meant that while what was visible remained much the same, what lay below the surface, in the invisible realms of our faith and our relationship with God at a more basic, gut level, now had more room and scope to accommodate the realities of what was going on.

Going beyond the cliff, this dividing line between the firmness of our tangible experience and the groundless space beyond the limits of reason, was hard. It was never something that was going to be possible completely voluntarily. Only the painful impetus of suffering compelled us to jump, but we did jump, and found new ground beneath our feet. Anger was the passage to that new land. Anger was allowed to run outwards and upwards: out of us, therefore leaving the place where it might conceivably have laid like a poison or a festering wound, and upwards to the only place and person that could accommodate it and turn it into something positive and life-giving.

NOTE

1   Paul Tournier, *Creative Suffering*, London: SCM Press 1982.

~IV~

A brave new world emerged beyond
The café houses of the Fulham road.
A new edifice of life and death
Kept separate. A neat device
Of space and stone to keep the rest
Of urban sprawl and hum enticed
By now and unaware of then or when –
Or this very now, where your emergent life spends
Its pulsing, bleeping, wired up hours
Beyond the sentried double doors.

The escalators were our journey,
Up yet down, out yet in,
Close to your edge, closer to learning
Of death in life and life from death emerging...

~4~

Death

Jesus, once more deeply moved, came to the tomb.
John 11.38

When we returned to London Jacob was immediately taken into hospital for what we thought would be a short stay, simply to sort out his digestive issues. Our assumption at that stage remained that Jacob had Pearson's syndrome. His visit to hospital was simply to get him sorted nutritionally and to have a small operation to fit a device that would enable him to have ongoing blood transfusions. However, while we were on holiday we had heard from our consultant that he had received a confusing result. His final and decisive diagnostic test for Pearson's syndrome had come back negative. He assured us that this probably meant that Jacob had a rare, possibly unknown form of the syndrome which would not be picked up by any current test. Despite his confidence we, as any parents would, quietly registered this news as hopeful.

It was during those two weeks in hospital that Jacob hit rock bottom. He had an operation to insert a Port-a-Cath into his side. This small device would enable him to have ongoing blood transfusions without the constant need to find a vein, something that is very difficult with small children. After that operation, which left him exhausted and weak, he picked up an infection that challenged him further. For those few days after the operation he lay motionless and emotionless in a small cot. He was monitored continuously, and the room in which he lay filled with the classic metronomic bleeps of a serious medical situation. He was fed through a tube that went down to his stomach via his nose. Various attempts to get him to feed through a bottle or out of a cup failed. He was at his most lifeless point. He was also at his most medicalized point. And while there was never any real sense that his life was in danger this was, on reflection, the time at which death seemed closest and appeared to enter the scene like a spectre more than at any other time, before or after.

It was a strange and almost surreal time. We were completely at the mercy of the hospital staff. Almost all normal parental responsibilities were now handed over to the professionals. We could change nappies and feed him through a tube but most of the time we felt like ancillaries in the care of a patient who was now owned by the hospital. This odd arrangement led us to feel like spectators watching from the outside, as Jacob's life ebbed and flowed at the mercy of monitoring devices, drugs and doctors. The room in which Jacob spent this time was almost unreal, even fictional. It was like a scene in a film to which we kept returning over and over again.

This was an experience of lifelessness and death, where the living being of our son was taken from us in every way, apart from the fact of his physical existence in that room. I realized then what a complex thing death is. It is not the black and white concept that our dichotomous language makes it out to be. Jacob's bleeps and breathing, his stirring and staring, continued to assure us of life beneath the surface. Yet in many ways at the surface was the visible presence of death. Death dominated where life, despite the symptoms of illness, had always done. But then that is reality. We live, all the time, somewhere between life and death. Most of the time life dominates to the extent that we can pretty much ignore death. During those two weeks, however, that room not only represented, but seemed to contain, the very things of death: a draining of the soul and personality of our son, a deterioration of his physical life and an enforced separation from him.

This state is a very uncomfortable one to live in. The temptation to ignore it is acute – or at least to dull the senses or find distraction. This we discovered in those days in and

around the hospital. The hospital itself was relatively newly
built and architects had taken the opportunity to construct the
hospital on an innovative basis. Like so many modern build-
ings, the hospital was centred round an atrium, a vast amphi-
theatre the length and height of the entire building. The
common experience of entering a hospital was completely
turned on its head, as here you came from busy, noisy streets
into this big, beautiful, bright space which hummed with a
certain degree of calm and tranquillity. There were no wards
at ground level; this area was given over to cafés and offices
and art. Art played an important role in the life of the hospital.
On occasions lunchtime concerts would take place and patients and visitors alike would gather to hear a jazz quartet or
a pianist. The walls were covered in newly commissioned art
and in one or two of the smaller atrium spaces, removed from
the central area, huge sculptures had been placed that filled
each space from top to bottom with colour and form.

In essence, great effort and thought had been applied to
make the central space of the hospital an extremely pleasant
and enriching place to be, and it had been achieved to great
effect. It was in stark contrast with most hospitals, where you
cannot wait to be free from the smell and sight of them. Here
you could almost forget you were in a hospital. You could sit
in the café and enjoy a surprisingly good cup of coffee, while
the reality of the hospital above you carried on invisibly. From
time to time a patient might be wheeled past in a wheelchair,
or walk past pushing a stand with a drip attached, but
essentially this space allowed you to forget where you were
and why you were there.

Beyond the doors of the hospital lay one of the most
salubrious and well-known streets in London. It had embraced the current trend for café culture and juice bars. Every
shop existed to serve the need to dispose of the large amount
of surplus capital that sloshes about in certain areas of
London. Antique shops, art shops, bars, restaurants, cafés,
home furnishing shops, all of them seemed to pander to the
need to live life to the full, to fill our homes with possessions

and enjoy ourselves. It was an intoxicating place. We drifted about in it feeling alien and removed, wanting in a sense to lose ourselves in it, yet constantly being tugged from behind by a long and slender thread that led us back to a first-floor ward, through security doors, into a room where our son lay. So we would drag ourselves, after an hour in a pleasant café, along the street buzzing with normal, happy, affluent life, through the revolving doors, up the escalator, along the corridor and into that room. It was a journey of just a few minutes but it seemed to traverse the whole chasm between life and death, heaven and hell.

If you ignore it for long enough it might just go away...
This whole surreal set-up seemed to serve as a huge metaphor for our general attitude and approach to death and suffering. While the drab and miserable environment of the classic Victorian hospital provides a particularly unpleasant experience for both patient and visitor, there is no disguising the contrast between the world outside and the inside of the hospital. We know when we enter such a place that we take a step closer to illness and death, and hence a step closer to confronting the potential or reality of illness and death in ourselves. In the hospital we found ourselves in, architecture and art had combined to dull this contrast almost to extinction. You could walk past that hospital and not notice it was there. You could go inside and feel blissfully unaware that such a place contained sad and tragic circumstances of the stuff of life and death; old people slowly eaten away by cancer, babies born on the cusp of life, or with no life at all, and ordinary people fighting for life and against death in wards somewhere above the atrium and out of view. There was undoubtedly something life-enhancing about the investment in art and music in that space, but we had the feeling that the reality of death was evaded, pushed to one side and out of sight, deliberately and effectively.

Perhaps, though, there is a perfect logic in this approach. It is tempting to interpret this as an architectural expression of a wider attitude that pervades our whole society. We live in a society that is deeply uncomfortable with death. For many the experience of that hospital mirrors a more profound attitude and response to death. A response that essentially avoids it, makes it invisible, shuns it, and basically does everything possible to pretend it isn't there. But we cannot avoid death, nor can we avoid the realities of dealing with death and loss. But the process of death and the ambiguous shades of darkening grey before the black of death we struggle to cope with. This is why treating life and death as a black-and-white issue is so attractive: the black of death can be ignored. Until, that is, it descends upon us in a great sweep, darkening everything for an intense and traumatic phase when someone dies and is laid to rest.

We are in essence deeply ambiguous in our attitude towards death. In one way we act as if it is nothing at all, and in another as if it matters immensely. Some months ago the media made much of the resignation of a hospital manager who had been held responsible for a situation where dead bodies had been stored in the hospital chapel. There was widespread outrage at the way the dead had been treated. The image of mortuary bags piled in a chapel rather than neatly stored in a mortuary was almost universally condemned and the manager was quick to resign his post. However, reflection in the days that followed revealed a growing sympathy with his decision, taken in what were surely difficult circumstances. One commentator in particular concluded that the episode demonstrated how ambiguous we are in our attitude to death and the dead. We shun death itself and yet show an enormous respect for the dead. That all this took place in a hospital where death is present there for all to see was perhaps particularly poignant.

Similarly in Alex Garland's book *The Beach*, and the film that was subsequently made of it, the ambiguity of our approach to death is brilliantly conveyed. *The Beach* is an exotic arcadia, an inaccessible beach in Thailand, invisible from the sea, on which a select group of enlightened travellers have built a community, divorced from the real world and free from its pressures. Life is a simple routine of fishing, gardening and cooking in order to resource the fun of afternoons spent playing football on the beach and evenings smoking dope and hanging out. As the story progresses it becomes more and more evident that the community is built on little else except the need to maintain this blissful state. Slowly the tension mounts, as this desperate need to preserve both the secrecy of the community to the outside world and the blissful utopian experience that it provides for those who live there begins to conflict with events. Gradually the community is invaded by the realities of the modern world and the human condition. There is danger encroaching from outside, a growing fear of others finding the island and the hidden community, and a threat from inside as illness, conflict and death break the calm surface of their lives together.

The demise of the community begins when two Swedish members are attacked by sharks during a fishing trip. One of the Swedes dies fairly quickly. His swift burial is crucial in order for the community to move on and return to normality. In the film this is portrayed as a classic non-religious but spiritual event where the community gather to pay their last respects in whatever way they choose. Many don quasi-religious trappings, wearing garlands of flowers that are then placed in the grave. Another member plays a plaintive tune on a recorder to create the sort of religious atmosphere that we all associate with funerals. However, when this is all over there is still the ugly and painful reality of the other Swede, who is slowly and agonizingly bleeding to death. He is consigned to a tent to 'recover'; the vast majority of the community avoid him, failing to visit him. Only a small band of friends pay any attention to him. In an evil twist to the story the hero, whose character is now so unstable that he lurches from sense to recklessness and horror with abandon, is made out as a figure of great compassion when he suffocates the Swede to death.

These are just two examples but they seem to concur with a general sense within modern western society that we are struggling to know how to deal with death. We no longer have a unifying principle or underlying foundation that begins to make sense of the process of death, death itself and whatever happens afterwards. Therefore we come up with a mixture of responses that generally deal with only one phase at a time: dying, death and the after-life. Very often there is then a disjunction between the response to one and the response to another. We are willing to venerate and spiritualize the dead in respect perhaps of some vague sense of their continued existence in some form, but the way we treat the dying and suffering is often at the other end of the scale. We treat old people with derision rather than respect, feeling that they have nothing more to offer our society other than being a source of knowledge of generations past and a reminder of a phase of life that we will probably have to go through at some stage.

A unified theory of death?
Modern society may treat religion, certainly organized religion, with scepticism and distrust, but it is still willing to turn to the religions when it comes to the subject of death. If anybody is going to have a sensible, balanced approach to death in our society, surely it is the religious – who for many exist only for those critical points of life that require a sense of otherness: birth, marriage and death. Yet my experience of the more assured evangelical end of the Christian theological spectrum hadn't fully prepared me for the face-to-face visit of death during those two weeks. My response was much like everyone else's: to ignore, to find distraction from the painful reality of what was going on inside that little room, and to hope that death would evade us, pass by on the other side and move on. This was not at the time a conscious decision – I was running purely on a minute-by-minute basis. It is probably the only way to live in that kind of situation. Months later, when I began to write about those experiences, I realized what lay at the heart of my reactions and response. In the weird spectrum of feelings that I sensed as I passed from the street, where

normality carried on regardless, to that hospital room, where life remained suspended and death hung in the air, was an unconscious and unrehearsed wrestling with the difficult and delicate subject of death.

It occurred to me then that nobody within the church, from a pulpit, in discussion or through any other medium, had really prepared me for dealing with death. Not death in the sense of that final state at the end of life, for I had had plenty of theology from a host of sermons that imparted confidence and hope in a very real and beautiful heavenly after-life, but in the sense of dying. Of the state that my son was in, caught closer to death than life, living and yet dying.

Surely, however, that's where we all are: in the same suspended position, but not necessarily of course at exactly the same point. We are all somewhere in the continuum between the black vacuum of death and the enormous rich and colourful place that Jesus described as 'life in all its fullness'. And if that is the case, if what was contained in that hospital room was not an abnormality, an errant situation that we would move on from and forget, but really a visible intensification of the reality of all of our lives, why had nobody addressed this for me before? Was this ambiguity towards death that the very architecture of the hospital seemed to communicate perhaps also expressed in the teaching of the sturdy biblical churches that I had grown up in, where death was catered for while dying was avoided? A Russian Orthodox speaker giving a lecture on the subject of suffering remarked that we spend too much time on the resurrection and too little time on the crucifixion. In other words, we spend more time rejoicing the victory of the resurrection and the hope of an after-life than the gritty realities of the process of dying with all its pain and blood.

Death is nothing...?

My experience of Christian teaching has leaned heavily in favour of the cross as a means to salvation, without exploring the cross as a point in history that reflects our own suffering. It has also been biased towards the cross as a mere precursor to the real stuff of the resurrection – victory over death and therefore hope for ourselves that we too will conquer death and find eternal life on the other side. That theology remains at the foundation of my own faith. And it was a genuine source of hope during those days when death came closest and rattled the surety of my own belief that death was not the end. For Emily this promise of hope became more real and tangible than ever before and the day-to-day struggles with death were put into some perspective by the promise of an eternal life free of its effects. Suddenly for her the promise of heaven really mattered; it took on a present urgency and relevance that perhaps it hadn't had before.

Yet somehow there had to be more. There had to be room in my theology and in my faith for some way of dealing with the imminent and very present effects of death. To me the focus on resurrection tended to nullify the pain of present-day death altogether. It could, if not tethered to the earthiness of pain and grief, simply lead us into a transcendent state of rather meaningless hope – hope based on nothing more than platitudinous rubbish uttered in a soothing voice. That sort of nonsense results in us comforting those who mourn with mellifluous statements, assuring them that death is just a door into heaven, that the deceased is now with the Lord, that in fact we shouldn't mourn because the deceased is in a better place.

This sort of theology is Christianity's equivalent of *The Beach*, where the dead are launched quietly and serenely to a better place while the dying, those left in the mire of present-day death, are left unattended and uncared for. Such a theology may well be reflected in this poem written in the early part of the twentieth century by Henry Scott Holland, then Canon of St Paul's Cathedral:

Death is nothing at all
I have only slipped away into the next room.
I am I and you are you.
Whatever we were to each other that we are still.
Call me by my old familiar name, speak to me in the
    easy way which you always used.
Put no difference into your tone; wear no forced air of
    solemnity or sorrow.
Laugh as we always laughed at the little jokes we
    enjoyed together.
Play, smile, think of me, pray for me.
Let my name be ever the household word that it always
    was.
Let it be spoken without effect, without the ghost of a
    shadow on it.
Life means all that it ever meant.
It is the same as it ever was; there is absolutely unbro-
    ken continuity.
What is this death but a negligible accident?
Why should I be out of mind because I am out of sight?
I am but waiting for you, for an interval, somewhere
    very near, just around the corner.
All is well.[1]

That poem was written after the First World War when British
people struggled to cope with the sheer scale of death in their
midst. There is undoubtedly some sympathy to be had for it,
as an attempt to react positively to the pain and grief of an
entire nation. Yet it also represents a failure to face up to the
pain and misery of death, casting it as nothing, to soothe those
who were having to deal with so much of it.[2]

Similarly such platitudes are the sort of theology that led
C. S. Lewis to write with such venom:

It is hard to have patience with people who say 'There
is no death' or 'Death doesn't matter'. There is death.
And whatever is matters. And whatever happens has

consequences, and it and they are irrevocable and irreversible. You might as well say that birth doesn't matter.[3]

What use were such platitudes in the intensity of his grief after losing his wife? What had happened had happened and he didn't need some soothing theology of the future that mentioned only the hope of heaven for his wife, and indeed for him. He needed a theology that dealt with the pain of his grief in the present.

Confronting death

I guess in the end I concluded that I had been forced to face up to death. I did this in retrospect rather than in the present. I continue to do it; it is not a stage that I pass through, a course that I complete, but an ongoing process. I am forced now to face up to it perhaps a little more intensely than most. Jacob, though now a fit, healthy and vibrant two-year-old, has a life expectancy half that of his peers. He is a potentially vulnerable child and each time that vulnerability gets the better of him he runs the risk of deterioration, in his lungs particularly. In a sense, then, with that very real vulnerability always with us, we live with death around a very much nearer corner than most.

I am comforted to find that there is in the Bible the raw material of a theology that does confront death. The story of the raising of Lazarus, in particular (John 11.1–44), shows that God does not think death nothing at all, far from it. Jesus, having delayed his return to the house of Mary and Martha, is now, not surprisingly, arriving to find Lazarus is dead. A full-blown Jewish wake is in progress, with the house packed with friends and family. Professional mourners provide a steady dirge of wailing. Everyone is crying at Lazarus' death. Finally Jesus arrives and asks, 'Where have you laid him?' He is brought to the tomb and the simple and profound statement recorded by John gives us his reaction: 'Jesus wept'.

Many have speculated why Jesus cried. If he cried out of loss, that seems odd – he has already declared to his disciples that 'Our friend Lazarus has fallen asleep; but I am going there to wake him up.' If he cried out of pain at the reality of death in the world then this is in some contrast to his other confrontations with it, such as the raising of Jairus' daughter, which seemed effortless almost to the point of playfulness. Philip Yancey speculates that the prayer that Jesus utters prior to Lazarus' resurrection lends evidence that his tears were an expression of the deep pain[4] Jesus felt at the state of the world – a world riddled with death, yet one where the promise of life was achievable. As the son of God, sent to model and invite people into that life, Jesus very much recognized how this balanced state of two worlds in one pivoted around him and the death that he knew he would have to face.

> At that very moment Jesus himself hung between two worlds. Standing before a tomb stinking of death gave a portent of what lay before him in this damned – literally damned world. That his own death would also end in resurrection did not reduce the fear or the pain. He was human: he had to pass through Golgotha to reach the other side.[5]

Even Jesus himself, with the divine perspective afforded to him, confronted death with fear and pain, expressed so humanly it must have been almost embarrassing. For Jesus, capable of effortlessly raising the dead as though death really were nothing, even a three-day-old, reeking corpse, death was really something. It caused him to mourn and express the emotions of anguish like you or me, indeed every human who has ever walked the face of this death-ridden earth.

Death a blessing?
So finally, then, does it stop there? Do we simply comfort ourselves with the revelation that at least God himself is not indifferent to death, that he feels what we feel, and when we

mourn in a sense he mourns with us? While that is a real comfort and a reflection of a God with us, rather than being aloof from the reality of death, there is surely more.

For me our experience of death, in the sense that I have talked about it, was not an experience devoid of benefit. It was not simply an episode that we endured and then left behind. Death for me was disarming, totally and utterly. When death confronts you and you are prepared to confront it you cannot fail but be disarmed by it. Death forces you to leave behind all pretensions of immortality – that life will somehow go on and on as it always has. Death forces us to appreciate that we are small, laughably vulnerable creatures. While we are capable of the most extraordinary things, from giant beautiful hospitals stocked with life-saving technology to complex cities that exhibit what vibrant, creative people we are, we are still essentially fragile, prone to breaking, prone to mortality. Confronting death can therefore have the effect of lengthening the dimensions of our lives. The scope of life increases and the third dimension, life's richness, likewise.

Jacob's brush with death makes his life more extraordinary in a way, and our gratitude for his presence in our lives is impressed upon us all the time. His vulnerability means that we rejoice that much more in his good health and in his life. Death therefore has a way of bringing life, of being a life-giving process, provided we are prepared to confront it and yield in some way to its life-giving potential.

This has been the experience of others. C. S. Lewis's reflections at the loss of his wife slowly begin to tease out the promise of life from her death. Perhaps death in a strange way has a retrospective way of enriching life. His wife, Joy, had expressed in her latter days, when the couple understandably squeezed every last drop of life out of the time they had left, that the 'grieving then was part of the joy now'. And so C. S. Lewis concludes that 'bereavement is a universal and integral part of our experience of love'.[6] It is a statement that seems to turn time on its head. But then perhaps if more of us contemplated and confronted our future death, and that of others, it would allow the enriching effect of death to make its impact now.

That impact also has the potential to be shared with others. It is not just our willingness to confront our own death that benefits us, but that benefit, that fruitfulness, has the potential to enrich others. As Henri Nouwen began to contemplate his own death he began to see that death was something that could be done 'well'. And in so doing, death could be of immense blessing to others:

> There is a blessing hidden in the poverty of dying. It is the blessing that makes us brothers and sisters in the same Kingdom. It is the blessing we receive from others who die. It is the blessing we give to others, when our time to die has come. It is the blessing that comes from a God whose life is everlasting.[7]

No wonder then that John ends the story of Lazarus not triumphantly but with a death knell. The whole story ends with a scene of restoration, Jesus reclining at the table with the resurrected Lazarus. Mary, ever the contemplative and the spiritually intuitive of the two sisters, pours a pint of pure nard over Jesus, nard that was, in Jesus' own words, saved 'for the day of my burial' (John 12.7). From the triumph of Lazarus' resurrection we are immediately thrown back towards death, this time that of Jesus himself.

But perhaps Mary gives us the first sign of our response to that death: that of worship. For it is in Jesus' death that we see most clearly the blessing of death. In Jesus' death we see the necessity of a passage through death in order for us to truly grasp life. Perhaps Jesus himself needed convincing of that. The confrontation at the tomb of Lazarus was what he, as a human being, needed, in order for him to utter, amidst the beads of bloody sweat and utter anguish, 'but not my will but yours be done'. Jesus was now finally prepared to die the death that was necessary in order for the full blessing of life to be unleashed upon the earth.

Ultimately that death gives us all we need to face up to death in the here and now. For in the death of Jesus the many facets of death that we are capable of splitting apart come together. In the death of Jesus on the cross our own struggles with dying, death and the after-life coalesce into one. For in that death God showed his empathy with our ever-present experience of dying and the event of death and thus opened up a way into the experience of eternal life, free forever from death. In the cross, therefore, Jacob's death, lurking continually under the surface, finds a comfort and a hope. We do not need to cast death off as nothing in order to face up to the reality of his struggle, but then nor do we feel the need to live in some unreal state of near-resurrection. The cross that held Jesus somehow holds our experiences together. They are no less painful for being held, but they are held closely against the presence of genuine empathy and genuine hope, and somehow that makes all the difference.

NOTES

1 Henry Scott Holland, 'What is Death?', in *Facts of Faith*, 1919.
2 It has also been suggested that the poem was actually written to knock down precisely the position it sets up. It is not therefore a position the author advocates.
3 C. S. Lewis, *A Grief Observed*, London: Faber and Faber 1961.
4 The Greek words translated 'deeply moved' in John 11.33 imply raw emotions such as anger or even rage.
5 Philip Yancey, *The Jesus I Never Knew*, London: Harper-Collins 1999, p. 180.
6 C. S. Lewis, *A Grief Observed*, London: Faber and Faber 1961, p. 43.
7 Henri Nouwen, *Our Greatest Gift*, London: Hodder & Stoughton 1994, p. 46.

~V~

Each night the amber-glow of city-dark
Drove us home on empty,
And the barometer at Holland Park
Read you with its pulse of electricity
Belting through liquid cobalt blue.
A number in the evening gloom
To mull over with overtones of doubt
And superstition, music loud, to keep the grieving out.

Silent then, we passed it needing
Nothing more than this abstract reading
In the dark. Like a random card
Dealt out, that filled the void
As large as need could afford
And as small as faith could discard.

5

Delay

Lord, if you had been here, my brother would not have died.
John 11. 21, 32

There is nothing like waiting to make a short time seem long and a long time seem like a lifetime. Waiting, with all its paradoxical characteristics of hope and despair, faith and doubt, had been a major feature of the entire journey so far with Jacob. But in the next phase of our journey this is what we seemed to spend all our days doing, waiting. Jacob was almost perpetually in the hands of others and our role in the whole drama was little more than that of two people at a bus stop waiting for the drone of an engine to build over the horizon. We were powerless and dependent, left to do nothing but wait out the hours, days and weeks as Jacob's health ebbed and flowed.

Within the grand wait of the entirety of Jacob's illness, when at times we were even unsure what we waited for (was it full recovery, full health, death or something in between?), there were significant and defined points that we waited for. Initially we waited for a diagnosis. We went back and forth from our local hospital as Jacob got more and more ill, until finally we entered that fateful room to be given the news that he had a rare condition known as Pearson's syndrome. There is no doubt that in some respects this was the worst point in our whole journey. Yet the end of every period of waiting brings relief, because at last you know and the future is no longer about whether you will ever know. It is no longer anything between the best to the worst case scenario. The future is now tangible. At last you know what you are dealing with.

Then we waited again. Doubt was cast over the Pearson's diagnosis, as a final diagnostic test came back negative. Jacob then hit rock bottom in terms of his physical health and we were once again thrown into the gap between the rosy and the gory scenarios that might mark out Jacob's future. Once again we clung disproportionately to comments that gave us hope. One consultant mentioned in passing that he had seen children come in diagnosed with Pearson's go home perfectly well. It was only a passing comment but I can hear him saying it even now. On the other hand, each of us held within ourselves our deepest fears, unsaid and yet somehow known to both of us.

Gradually a diagnosis began to emerge. Jacob had been tested for cystic fibrosis (CF) before but really only to eliminate it as a possibility. Every time they did the test on him it didn't work properly and results were inconclusive. While some of his symptoms might have pointed towards CF, those that were of greatest concern to the doctors were highly unusual in CF patients. Jacob's unusual symptoms had thrown our initial set of doctors off the trail and in the meantime he had become extremely ill. Eventually, however, the riddle began to unravel itself. Finally one consultant sat with us and said he would eat his hat if Jacob did not have CF. Even then the last remnants of hope that he would be wrong remained with me until finally we were given conclusive proof that this was it, the future for Jacob and for us was CF.[1]

We received the news with very mixed emotions. There was relief that the wait was genuinely over and we finally knew what we were dealing with. This was tinged with some degree of joy, since after all this was not the worst case scenario. Pearson's *had* been our worst case scenario. From a position of facing a future where our son would never have got better, never have walked, never led anything like a normal life, we could allow ourselves to envision a future where Jacob did all that any parent hopes for and looks forward to. Jacob would walk, he would talk, he would go to school and most likely he would grow up and become an adult. At the same time, though, CF remained a hard return for all our waiting. Emily knew a friend her own age with CF. She knew what CF meant, and the hard times that she and her parents had been through. Life with CF was never going to be easy.

So with the reality of a future dominated by this condition settling uncomfortably into our lives we moved hospitals with Jacob and set out on the road of getting him well enough to return home. This move seemed a formality; after all, now that the problem had been solved Jacob could be treated accordingly and he would soon recover. Perhaps this was what made the waiting of this next phase hardest of all. We knew, at least in theory, what our future with Jacob was going to be like and we just wanted to be allowed to get on with it. We wanted to get Jacob home, knowing that life wasn't going to be easy, yet wanting to move on and face those challenges. We were made to wait, however, and in this period of waiting, characterized by frustration more than by anxiety, we experienced perhaps our most testing time of delay.

Living in delay
We had thus lived through three periods of waiting. First we waited for an initial diagnosis, then we repeated that process and waited for another. Finally we waited for Jacob to become well enough to come home. They were periods of suspension, of being caught in the realms of infinite possibility and of the unknown. Most of us live our lives in a state of knowing and of journey. In other words, most of the time we know the situation and the ingredients of our life, what we will do tomorrow, next week, even next year. We plan for the future with an agreeable degree of certainty and the ground beneath our feet feels solid and dependable. Our lives have direction because we know where we are going. Even if we don't we can at least have a good go at predicting it. Having this state stripped away feels abnormal to us; it feels vulnerable and frightening. We are no longer in control; instead we are dependent on others, on God, on fate, on chance. Suspension

forces us to rely on something other than our own abilities, our own power, our own capacity to forge our own futures.

Delay seems the best word to describe our state of experience for some six months. While the normality we grow accustomed to and generally enjoy is suspended, the dominant force within is a desire for things to return to normal or for things to be resolved or healed and made better again. Every day when this doesn't happen is another day of waiting and another day of delay.

Delay is also a very active state, because within it, with the symptoms of suspended normality around us, we actively wait. We do not wait passively with the assured calmness of someone who waits for a bus that is always on time. Instead we wait with the anxious energy of the person who waits for news from the operating theatre or from the battlefront. Delay is charged with emotion. Delay lays bare what we really feel and what we really believe. Delay forces us away from our independence and makes us choose what it is we do depend on.

We were people whose stated inclination was to depend on God. We did not believe that Jacob was now in the hands of fate but very much in the hand of God the Father. Our active state of delay forced us to express our dependence on God by praying to him. We believed that within this state of delay, in which we were powerless, we could call on an all-knowing, all-powerful God whose nature and heart led him to heal and restore. God would surely be the means by which our delay would swiftly end and normality be restored.

Praying in the delay

Yet our experience was far from this apparently defendable claim. There were many key points within the period of delay when it seemed plain to us that a simple intervention from God might well speed up the resolution and bring it to an end. Yet time and time again prayers appeared to go unanswered. We prayed passionately for Jacob to feed from a bottle instead of being fed through a tube. The idea of Jacob having a tube permanently inserted into his stomach through his nose seemed horrible to us. We felt it was important that when we took Jacob home we would be able to feed normally. Yet he never learnt to feed from a bottle and eventually came home with the feeding tube still attached.

We prayed that his operation, when he first went into hospital, would go smoothly and that he would recover quickly. Yet after the operation he contracted an infection that brought on the worst period of his illness. For weeks and weeks we prayed that his breathing would clear and that all the antibiotics they pumped into his bloodstream would be effective. Yet week after week the doctors would say that they couldn't understand why his chest wasn't improving, and the fact that it wasn't meant that he would have to stay in hospital for another week.

And of course right from the very beginning we prayed for his complete healing. We prayed in the times when we didn't know whether he would live or die that eventually we would be able to take him home and begin to look back on the whole episode as a bad start. We prayed for healing right the way through and we continue to pray now. In this sense the delay goes on and we continue to depend on God for a resolution to the state of illness in Jacob and an end to the delay. We are still waiting.

So what on earth was all that prayer all about? Why were so many prayers apparently unanswered and the delay allowed to go on? Were we expected to pray? Did it make any difference? Was there really any point in praying? I remain convinced that prayer is what we *have* to do in situations of delay. Not have to in the sense of being made to, but have to in the sense of being compelled to, of having nowhere else to turn. However, in delay we are faced with the possibility that this natural inclination, the humble broken dependence on God, is nothing more than meaningless shouting in the wind. It may make us feel better but ultimately it makes not a blind bit of difference. This is how it feels in the intense present moment somewhere in the midst of delay. We pray in the hope that we will see answers, healing and the end to our situation of abnormality, yet what we often get is more of the same. In that present moment, any present moment in the midst of continuing delay, nothing makes sense. The present tells us that because God hasn't acted he either does not exist, isn't who we thought he was, or just isn't listening.

This is often how it feels to pray in the delay. It is how Mary and Martha felt as their brother got sicker and sicker and eventually died. They waited an agonizing three days for Jesus to return, knowing from their own experience that he had the power to heal. His arrival on the scene would surely take away all their pain and restore Lazarus to health and their family to its former state. But Jesus failed to come and by the time he finally arrived it was too late. Lazarus had been dead for three days, and there was surely no hope now. And so both Mary and Martha, on apprehending Jesus when he finally arrived, utter the words, 'Lord, if you had been here, my brother would not have died.' Both utter them with degrees of confusion, hurt, disappointment and anger. For what they had experienced did not marry up with the Jesus that they knew. There was disjunction between the Jesus they thought they knew and the Jesus who had failed to help them when it mattered most.

This is the experience of delay – doubt, confusion, disappointment, anger, for some even a loss of faith. In delay the disjunction between the God we thought we knew and the God of our experience proves too much. Yet delay can also be a time of great growth and refinement, although often we only sense this in retrospect. Certainly for us the delays we faced, the waiting we endured, were a cocktail of all the emotions and feelings listed above. And yet I can sense now with my present perspective that that experience of waiting will remain one of the most enriching times of my life in terms of my understanding of God and my faith in him. This does not make delay or waiting any easier. I still struggle with all the same things that waiting invoked in me then. However, perhaps some reflections from that period of intense delay, when the need for God seemed so acute and thus his apparent failure to respond so disappointing, bring greater resilience and greater perseverance to the periods of delay that confront me now.

What are we praying for?

Now, just as then, I wonder what I pray for when I pray for Jacob. I remember being struck at the time, after Jacob's diagnosis of CF, at the willingness of many people to pray for Jacob's complete healing. For someone with a background in biochemistry this seemed just too big a prayer, a bridge too far, both for my prayers and for the God prayed to.

CF is a genetic condition. In every cell of his body at the molecular level, Jacob has a mistake. Just one silly little mistake. The swapping of one molecule for another. Yet the impact is enormous, life-changing. The all-pervasiveness and the profundity of Jacob's condition challenges my faith. It says that this is something written in indelible ink; it is part of who Jacob is. His genetic alphabet is just the slightest bit different from ours and that is just the way it is. Nothing, not even God, is capable of changing that.

Yet of course he is. The story of Lazarus, and others like it, continue to testify that even the most apparently hopeless situations are not hopeless. Death is after all the final frontier. After passing through it there is no return. This is life's great certainty. The indelibility of that full-stop in our lives is impossible to ignore. The timing of Jesus' arrival is therefore no accident in this respect. That he arrives a full three days late is stated so that we all know for certain that Lazarus is dead. Jewish tradition held that a person's spirit hovered over the physical body for three days. At any point during those three days it might be persuaded to re-enter the body and bring it back to life. After three days, however, the spirit left and any chance of resurrection was utterly gone. This made the resurrection of Lazarus that much more amazing to those who looked on. Jesus had done something that everyone knew, in their traditions and in their understanding of the world, was utterly impossible.

So why not Jacob? And why not pray for it? Well, absolutely, why not? But with a few caveats. There is a tendency within the church – and perhaps within the more triumphalist sections of it – to misunderstand what miracles are. There is a movement within the church that expects miracles, advertising them and feeding on them in a kind of frenzied state of excitement. It is a movement that seems to suggest that miracles of the Lazarus-raising kind should be part and parcel of our everyday experience. There is a corollary that suggests that if they are not, then that has something to do with our faith, or the lack of it.

Surely this is a fundamental misunderstanding of what miracles are. It suggests that miracles are the norm, when in fact they are the opposite. Miracles are not the natural course of events. They are unnatural events, or more accurately supernatural events. In these events the natural state of the world as we understand it is suspended and superseded. Can we honestly expect this to be part of our everyday experience? After all, even Jesus' miracles seemed to be squeezed out of him, either because of the faith of a person, the persistence of another, or simply Jesus' compassion. But they were not the norm; they were exceptions rather than the rule, as Philip Yancey articulates:

> Surely the baffling selectivity of miracles was no easier to understand in Jesus' day than it is today. A man who could walk on water did it only once. What self-restraint! Yes, he brought Lazarus back from death and dried the eyes of his sisters – but what about the many other sisters and wives and daughters and mothers who were grieving that day for their own loved ones? When Jesus himself discussed miracles directly, he stressed their *infrequency*.[2]

The painful reality is that many people have been destroyed by the huge disappointment brought on by an expectation that God would perform a miracle for them. How many have been hurt by confident statements by those around them, and within themselves, that a miracle would happen? Such statements have the potential to impress, to seem like Herculean feats in the Olympiad of faith, but in the intensity of delay and the failure of a miracle to arrive, the weight of expectation has the power to break us, not restore us.

Somehow then we have to be able to allow ourselves to live in the uncomfortable place of believing in the potential of miracles, in the omnipotence of God and the compassionate heart of God, and yet not allow that belief to dwell on whether that potential might be realized within our own lives. That we live in a time where miracles are infrequent bursts of the supernatural into our world is both painful and yet hopeful. Thus we hope for a miracle for Jacob, we even pray for a miracle for Jacob, but we recognize the infrequency of miracles and acknowledge that what is best for us may not be anything like what we expect.

Who does prayer change?

One of the classic questions of prayer is whether we are actually in the business of changing God's mind. Or to put it another way, is God in the business of having his mind changed? There would seem to be numerous examples in the Old Testament in particular when this was in fact the case. Abraham's ability to barter God down from fifty to ten righteous men in order to save the city of Sodom is frequently discussed (Genesis 18.16–33). Nevertheless we struggle with the tensions between our understanding of God as immutable and dependable and the suggestion that part of his character makes him seem almost fickle.

On the other hand there is very little attention paid to the other perspective. That prayer is about changing us, not changing God. On these thoughts I am indebted to some close friends who have experienced the pain and turmoil of delay. For some time they tried for a child but failed. They then went through four rounds of IVF before finally conceiving a beautiful daughter. For them their journey in prayer took them from the point of seeing prayer as 'what God can do for me' to 'what do you want of me?' When three rounds of IVF that had been prayed into by probably hundreds of people all failed, they had to question what exactly was going on when they and others prayed. When the fourth attempt succeeded, despite the fact that their physical, emotional and spiritual exhaustion left them unsure and unable to decide whether to pray or not, one has to ask what prayer is really about. Was it any coincidence that three unsuccessful rounds, that had brought them to the point of giving up, had then been followed by one that was successful? Is prayer more about our attitude towards God, our submission to God and our dependence on God, than the words we use, or the frequency or the zeal of our prayers?

Prayer changes us, within the refining conditions of delay, from 'Lord, this is what I want' to 'Lord, what do you want of me?' We are changed from an understanding of self that is so standard in our western culture, one of 'what's in it for me', to a situation of selflessness, abandonment and dependence rather than independence. This cuts to the heart of the human condition, to the nub of the issue of our fallen relationship with God. We have this intoxicating tendency towards independency, towards doing things the way we want to by ourselves and for the benefit of ourselves alone. When prayer carries us on a journey that descends into the depths of delay, that independency is dropped like a large unnecessary piece of luggage. And in casting it aside we begin to discover what dependency is all about.

This was a key revelation for Sheila Cassidy, the director of a hospice in Plymouth. She became well known in 1975 when she was arrested and tortured in Chile for treating a wounded revolutionary. It was this experience, during which she was placed in solitary confinement, that brought a profound revelation to her:

> Left to my own devices and with the constant harassment of the interrogators behind me I found that, for the first time since my arrest, I had sufficient emotional and intellectual space to manoeuvre, to choose what to

do. My immediate inclination was to scream out to God to help, to batter spiritually on the bars of my cage, begging to be released … Then a very curious thing suggested itself to me: while I knew it was quite right and proper to besiege heaven with my prayers to be released, an even better way would be to hold out my empty hands to God, not in supplication but in offering. I would say, not 'Please let me out', but, 'Here I am Lord, take me. I trust you. Do with me what you will.'[3]

For me I guess there are elements of both. Now I continue to pray for our liberation, and that of Jacob, from the pain and the injustice of his illness that is a part of our lives every day. Yet I am learning that while on the surface my prayers may sound like petition, pure and simple, underneath is a growing current that augments and complements this most basic prayer. This current is essentially attitudinal. While everything in me wants this situation to be resolved, for the pain to go away and normal life be restored, I am willing to be dependent and to submit to what God would want of me. Practically speaking much prayer is petition, but at its foundations and in its attitude it is submission, pure and simple. We are made as creatures who seek after God and ask of him the things we want as well as need. We are being made into creatures who are utterly dependent and submitted to what God would want of us.

Jesus spoke many words on prayer, and these form the basis for much of the way we pray and formulate our approaches towards God. Perhaps, however, he taught immeasurably more in his own tortuous prayer in the Garden of Gethsemane, which married the petition 'Father … take this cup from me' with the utterly dependent statement 'yet not my will, but yours be done' (Luke 22.42).

The prayers of others

Finally, we were acutely aware, as Jacob made tortuously slow steps towards recovery, and we continue to be so now, of the prayers of others. We were both amazed and incredibly touched at the number of people who prayed for a child they hardly knew. There were churches all over the country praying for our little boy on sometimes the flimsiest of connections. We even had a convent in Switzerland praying for him every day because of a connection with Jacob's great-grandmother.

What this suggests to me is that prayer is not the sole property of the individual and God. It is also about the worshipping community and God. This is really quite sensible. Communities come into their own when the constituent unit, usually the family, for whatever reason finds itself unable to cope or provide. If we are part of an interdependent community then we hope that if we fall ill, or if some misfortune befalls us, then that community will come to our aid. Similarly, when spiritually our resources are stretched the prayers of our community make good the resources that we lack.

This is a powerful and enriching process. We discovered the extraordinary support of the church, the community of God, at a time when our spiritual resources were stretched to the limit. It gave us confidence that though we were prayed out and our faith was severely tested, there were others who were in a sense faith for us. Similarly our friends on their fourth IVF attempt, when they were so spiritually exhausted and demoralized that they couldn't bring themselves to pray, sensed more keenly than ever the support and encouragement of the prayers of others.

The greatest illustration of this is surely the healing of the paralytic (Mark 2.1–12). In this well-known story a paralysed man is lowered down through the roof by four friends to Jesus' feet while he is in mid-sermon. Mark writes that 'when Jesus saw *their* [my italics] faith, he said to the paralytic, "Son, your sins are forgiven"' (Mark 2.5). I am not sure whether the word 'their' refers to all five men, that is, including the paralytic, or just the four friends. In imagining the feelings of the paralytic I see how we felt during that time, every day seeing a situation that never appeared to change and at the same time feeling faith seep away. How extraordinary and how liberating that the faith of others, the faith of these friends – who for all we know brought this man under duress because they were so convinced that Jesus could bring change – can bring those lacking in faith the restoration they so dearly want. It suggests a God of mercy who is out looking for the merest crumb of faith in connection with a situation of pain in order to bring healing, rather than a God who requires heroic faith in the individual. And it suggests the value of faith as an open community currency rather than one held individually and secretly.

So in prayer there is a process of change from independence to dependence and also *inter*dependence. The prayers of others force us into a place of interdependence, a humble place where we admit our own weaknesses and our deficiencies of faith. We face up to human frailty and the struggle of faith in a world where the miraculous happens, but not in our experience and not when we really need it to. This is, I think, not a bad place to be.

Delay's end

For many, delay ends with restoration. For others delay goes on and only the promise of heaven, when all will be restored, gives realistic hope of an end to all the waiting. It is important to realize that in a sense God waits too. Jesus weeps at Lazarus' tomb and on his entry to Jerusalem because he so wants the world to be restored, but knows that this has to wait. God longs for the restoration of his world and for a time when there will be no pain or death or suffering. Returning to the story of Lazarus once again, we have as clear a reason as we can hope for as to what delay is all about, and what if any end justifies the means of delay.

We have been told that even though Jesus heard that Lazarus was sick he stayed where he was for two more days. Within that time, which eventually resulted in Jesus arriving so long after Lazarus' death, we get two revealing statements from Jesus. On hearing that Lazarus is sick Jesus says, 'This sickness will not end in death. No, it is for God's glory so that God's Son may be glorified through it' (John 11.4).

Later, as the disciples worry about Jesus returning to the vicinity of Jerusalem, Jesus says: 'Lazarus is dead, and for your sake I am glad I was not there, so that you may believe' (John 11.14–15).

The depths of these statements are plumbed by delving into the meaning of the words 'glorified' and 'believe'. For when Jesus says that he might be glorified through what is about to happen he does not mean that he is about to receive acclaim or praise or recognition. What he means is that what is about to happen will happen in order that more of him might be revealed. Therefore, the second statement essentially says that Jesus is glad that he wasn't there to heal Lazarus, because his late arrival and the certainty of his death means that the miracle of Lazarus' resurrection will surely engender genuine belief (which in the Gospels always refers to the sort of belief we mean when we use the word 'faith') in the hearts of his disciples.

Miracles are indeed a response of a compassionate God to the suffering of the world. But there is a greater purpose in them that perhaps explains their infrequency and their elusiveness. They also reveal more of God to the recipients of the miracle and the community in which that miracle takes place. In the Gospels miracles continually resound with a greater significance, with a symbolism and aptness that would not have been lost on those who saw them or heard about them in first-century Palestine. The raising of Lazarus was a remarkable miracle for Lazarus and his family but it may have been harsh for other families also mourning that day. The greater work perhaps is the revelation that it was to the disciples then and the revelation it is for us now.

And so too for us. While delay may seem as illogical to us as Jesus' refusal to respond to Lazarus' sickness, the hard truth behind the confusion and the doubt is that delay is a revelatory process. Delay is one of God's ways of lovingly ensuring that we discover more about him. Delay lays us bare enough to force us to search beyond the comfortable place we had got to and to discover more. Our assumptions are cast aside, the structures we have erected in a familiar and perhaps static place are dismantled and we are compelled onwards. Delay is not as it would appear, the result of a diffident or callous God, or even of a God powerless to act. It is used lovingly by him to enable us to grow and discover.

The final agonizing and frustrating phase of waiting came to an end some six weeks after Jacob had been diagnosed with CF. He finally conquered an infection that had defied any antibiotics thrown at it, and he broke the physical and psychological milestone of five kilogrammes body weight. We took our photos of Jacob in his cot, which had been his station night and day for so long, packed up his things and drove him home. We were in a kind of dream, as though he were the rarest and most precious child in the world. He arrived home with a tube down his nose, although in a very cunning and typically Jacob-like manner he pulled it out two days later. And so we began to live again, rediscovering parenthood, rediscovering Jacob.

Life with Jacob is never comfortable. We live in the midst of delay all the time. At times things get hard, and the implications of his condition impose on him and on us more than at other times. We cry out in ways that Mary and Martha must have done, imploring Jesus to return. Yet we are richer for it. God is necessarily tangible and present. We are forever reminded of our dependence on him and on our interdependence within the community of God. We are seldom allowed to feel that our independence can suffice in the present reality of our world.

But then the reality of our world is that all of us live in delay. For the majority of the time most of us can be content with the world the way it is. And yet the world is in pain; it is crying out for Jesus to stop delaying and return. We are caught in suspension between death around us and the life of the kingdom of God, between present pain and future healing, between glimpses of the kingdom and the fullness of its revelation, and between Jesus' departure and his return, when finally the waiting will be over.

NOTES

1	CF is a genetic condition that affects the way cells in our body balance water across their cell membranes. In CF patients this balancing act is disrupted and in many cell types this causes severe problems. In particular CF sufferers very often cannot digest fat because the pancreas cannot deliver the appropriate enzymes to the intestine. Perhaps most significantly, CF affects the lungs. The ability of the lungs to ward off infection is severely compromised and CF patients suffer from frequent chest infections and a gradual deterioration of lung function. Life expectancy for CF sufferers has gone up enormously over the past 30 years. At present a CF sufferer can expect to live on average 30–35 years.

2	Philip Yancey, *The Jesus I Never Knew*, London: HarperCollins 1999.

3	Sheila Cassidy, *Sharing the Darkness*, London: DLT 1988.

~VI~

This time last year was our spring
Hidden from all else, to us an opening.

Next year, like every year
The leaves will grow on different
Yet the same, and Autumn's purge
Will have disappeared
In a memory like a spent
Story at the whim of the journalist's urge.

This year, unlike the others
I study this massive murder,
This armageddon of the season
With a richer sense of pathos,
Like there is something deeper, further
in the fading veins and wilting-without-reason.

6

Rebirth

He who goes out weeping, carrying seed to sow, will return with songs of joy, carrying sheaves with him.

Psalm 126.6

Pain is a Holy Angel which shows treasure to man which otherwise remains hidden forever.

Adalbert Stifter[1]

A week or so ago I went to a Nigerian naming ceremony. This ceremony takes place soon after the birth of a new baby and brings together family and friends to pray over and bless the new arrival and his or her parents. In Nigerian culture names are of great significance, much more so than in British culture. They are chosen for their meaning. The ceremony was therefore a very real expression of the belief that we are born not by accident, but by design; not for some indiscriminate reason, but for a purpose. The naming of a child is not simply to distinguish that child from another in the playground, but in order to reflect the uniqueness, in God's eyes and in his divine plan, that sets that child apart.

In our culture, however, we are a little vain and nonchalant about names. Names are fashion items almost, reflecting trends or the latest soap character to grab our attention. We certainly gave our son the name Jacob predominantly because we liked it. No doubt we too were affected by the trend for slightly unusual names (thus making them common) and for slightly more adventurous biblical names. However, the more I observe Jacob and reflect on those definitive first months of his life and our lives with him, the more I think it was no coincidence that we named him as we did.

The name Jacob means literally 'he grasps the heel'. Isaac's son Jacob was second of a set of twins to emerge. He did so grasping the heel of his brother Esau, as though determined not to be overshadowed by the significance of his brother's status as firstborn. Figuratively Jacob also means 'schemer', and this is amply demonstrated throughout Jacob's life. Esau's birthright is gained by stealth as Jacob dupes his father into giving him his blessing. In another story Jacob's flocks increase impressively through an ingenious scheme of breeding.

Despite the rather naive way that we chose Jacob's name he appears to be showing, more and more, how appropriate that name is to him. It seems increasingly curious that our Jacob's first act, after emerging from the womb, was to grasp the scissors used seconds before to cut the umbilical cord. It required two midwives to wrest his little hands from them. As he grows up he continues to exhibit a developing cunning, a propensity to get his way by stealth and scheming, rather than the standard toddler's use of force.

But it is in another famous story from the biblical Jacob that this resonance begins to sound most deeply. In Genesis 32 Jacob wrestled all night with a man he did not know. When that man found that he could not overpower Jacob he touched Jacob's hip and it was dislocated. Yet in the pain of the struggle Jacob held on, determined to get a blessing from the stranger: 'I will not let you go unless you bless me,' he says (Genesis 32.26). With incredible boldness Jacob asks the man's name and receives a blessing. At that point Jacob is in no doubt as to the identity of the man for he names the place where this happened Peniel, which means 'face of God'. For there Jacob had wrestled with God face to face.

In this story is a connection that I believe is at the very heart of our lives and that of our own Jacob. That connection is one between pain and blessing. In the middle of a dark and lonely night of wrestling with a stranger Jacob feels a sharp and intense pain as his hip is wrenched from its socket. The reflex reaction must surely have been to release and tend to his own pain, to submit defeat and give up the fight. Or, perhaps more understandably, complain and disengage, accusing the man of using foul play. Whatever this wrestling was about it would seem that the tactics employed by the man had now turned dirty. Instead Jacob, the schemer, hangs on in the almost illogical belief that there is a blessing to be had. Pain does not shift Jacob from this belief – on the contrary, it appears to strengthen it – and finally he gets not only a blessing but also a new name. God bestows on Jacob a new identity which defines him further. This new identity suggests that this all-night wrestling match was a rite of passage for Jacob, a process of accelerated transformation that left Jacob so changed that he required a new name. Pain for Jacob becomes a life-changing, life-enhancing event.

Tears and joy
Someone, at some time after Jacob's diagnosis with CF and during our long stay in hospital, gave us this verse: 'He who goes out weeping, carrying seed to sow, will return with songs of joy, carrying sheaves with him' (Psalm 126.6).

It was a verse that immediately had a deep resonance with us, although I didn't fully understand it then. I guess I understand it only partially now. But somehow I knew it was one of those verses from the Bible that was worth exploring. Perhaps what convinced me it was more than just one of those platitudinous offerings that people sometimes bring was a single word at the heart of the verse: the word 'will'. That may seem strange, but at the time we were desperate for anything that might speak to us in order to enlighten our future. What we were in the midst of seemed like a perpetual and uncomfortable present. Life was lacking a future that showed any change from the present. Life was extremely painful and it did not appear to be getting any better. While those two months in hospital seems a short time now, then it seemed interminably long.

In one sense time disappeared altogether. I was oblivious of the seasons and sometimes uncertain of the day of the week, and the interior of the hospital changed little. Most of the occupants of the other beds in the ward came and went relatively quickly, while Jacob remained in his familiar spot. Our lives were completely focused on Jacob, getting him better and getting home. But he appeared to be failing to get better and the prospect of some kind of future where he was healthy and at home became less and less realistic. In that eternal, monotonous present our world was a small and increasingly hopeless one. We began to lose sight of a world beyond the hospital and of a world where Jacob was no longer ill. In some ways this was one of the hardest points of our journey, because although we knew his diagnosis and he was not clinically at his worst, visible signs of improvement were virtually non-existent. We realized clearly and intensely that it is not necessarily our circumstances that cause us to feel pain to a greater or lesser extent, but the degree to which those circumstances show signs of improvement. For us, our world lost sight of hope. It got to be a very small place with little joy. In our painful futurelessness we gradually lost the dynamic of hope – a dynamic that is so intimately connected to happiness.

This is the corrosive potential of pain. It has the power to shrink us, to pull us inwards, so that we think there is nothing but the present and any hope of a meaningful future is gone. Psychologically we shorten our scope. When we are happy and content, when we have things to look forward to and a positive present connected to that hopeful future, the scope of our existence is wider. It has room for work, for friends, for community, for initiative, for spontaneity and creativity. But often pain and unhappiness cause us to retreat inwards, to close up, and makes us defensive and childlike. We become hopelessly and passively dependent on whatever may happen to us. We lose any power to influence our circumstances.

Into this context the word 'will' came. Previous to this all my hopeful futures had been dashed. When Jacob became ill I hoped for a future where he got better and everything was fine. Twice I had hoped for a simple and benign solution to all his problems and twice we had received diagnoses that suggested a life-long struggle. Even after diagnosis I had hoped for a speedy recovery and a swift return to normality. Instead we continued to have setbacks. He continued to struggle to put on weight, to the confusion of the medical staff. At one point he was also overdosed on his antibiotics. While no lasting damage was done, nevertheless it felt like the last straw at the time. There was scarce evidence of progress. All our hopeful futures had failed to materialize.

However, this was a very different kind of 'will', a very different kind of future. All those previous futures were based on one thing, that of being released from the physical and experiential reality of the pain we found ourselves in. In this sense pain was just a miserable thing we had to go through, nothing more. We would hang on grimly and resolutely until it was past and then carry on. We hoped that the pain would go tomorrow, and if it didn't we hoped that it would go the day after that. It is our inherent reaction as human beings to wish to rid ourselves of pain's effects. After all, isn't this the future we are headed for, a world without pain? If so, then pain is of another age, and while it may linger in this age, it has no place and no power in the present. Surely God has dealt with pain? While we are yet to experience fully the freedom that brings, surely pain is essentially defeated?

This verse suggested something different. It said pain and joy are encapsulated within a creative process, one described by the metaphor of sowing and reaping. This process involves not only the positive side of our emotional experience but also the painful, tearful side. In fact the process itself begins with pain and tears. It begins when weeping and pain do not result in us shrinking inwardly or curling into a corner until the pain goes away. It begins instead when we go out with the pain, when we 'go out weeping'. What can this possibly mean?

At one level this highlights the contrast between two very different reactions to pain. One is passive, the other active. One says that pain is just the way it is, something to be endured and ignored, the other says there is something positive and worthy about pain. The former reaction would seem to be the most common. We are not as articulate as we might be in dealing with our own pain and that of others. And because we feel challenged by pain, and threatened at our inability to deal with it psychologically, emotionally, and even theologically, we ignore it and shut down. Pain has the tendency to make us like modern lepers. It makes us inclined to remove ourselves from our community or society. Sometimes I think we respond to pain as we would to an air raid, sheltering in bunkers of our own making until everything has passed, then emerging back into the world as though nothing had happened and everything is fine. But pain cannot be ignored; it has to go somewhere. Often it goes inwards, and alongside the shrinking from and shirking pain is the process of containing that pain somewhere within us.

This verse suggests another reaction. Pain has something worthy about it, something potentially creative and transformational. We *can* 'go out weeping'. There is nothing to be ashamed of. We have not lost the potential to give and to contribute to the world we live in. On the contrary we have gained something. Pain is described as though it were something of great potential. It is like seed that we have the opportunity to sow, to cast liberally around. Imagine the action of going out to sow. We actively take ourselves from our homes, we walk, we move forward. And then in sowing we are forced to throw our arms from our bodies; the act of sowing is an act of unfurling. It is the perfect antidote, the precise opposite of the passive reaction of shrinking inwards and of internalizing pain. Going out weeping to sow is an act of defiance; it is also an act of faith. It says that there has to be something positive about pain. It says that pain is part of God's world, part of God's way of communicating and revealing himself. It suggests a refusal to allow pain to be corrosive and damaging, and a belief in the potential for transformation, if pain is used in the right way.

The verse goes on to suggest that the results of this process

will be joy. For me this was the key. Until that point all my
futures had been influenced by the ugliness and dreadfulness
of pain. They had been based on an assumption that the only
future for pain was its absence. The only hopeful future for us
was one without pain. And this was becoming harder to hold
on to, as such a future looked less and less likely. The reality
was that we had a son for whom pain would always be
present. For us too pain would never be far away. Now,
however, an alternative future suggested itself. Suddenly there
was the suggestion of a positive future despite the pain. In this
verse the future was not about freedom from pain but something completely different – joy. Joy is intimately connected
and related to pain, in the same way that seeds are connected
with the crops they produce. Without pain there was no joy
and a future without pain suggested a lost opportunity to reap
from the present experience of pain.

At that point there was a future again. I had been caught
in a tortuous circle of hoping for a future without pain when
the reality was that pain would be an ever-present part of our
lives. Pain was no longer something to ignore or resist but
something to engage with, confront, harness and put to use.
Furthermore, this was not some dispirited consequence of a
miserable reality, but actually a path to joy, perhaps a joy I had
never experienced before.

Pain – a positive process
It is extraordinary how often theology develops in order to
be imposed upon the circumstances we are facing, very often
in order to justify them. During apartheid the church in
South Africa was guilty of a theology that defended the
status quo. The church was just as racially divided and
discriminatory as the society around it. It is almost incredu-
lous, from our privileged point in time, to imagine how a
church could condone what was going on in South Africa
then, but when theology is developed in this manner it can
happen. Theology is not an experimental process, that we
use to defend or refute theories we already cherish about the

world we live in. Instead theology is a process of examination. We hold the word of God, and the character and principles of the Kingdom of God, against our circumstances and experiences in order to inform ourselves about them and perhaps change our attitudes and behaviour. We should be open to being challenged by the word of God to take on new understandings, ones that perhaps surprise and require something of us. Theology is a dangerous process, not a soothing one.

It was in this sense strange that having suddenly found this new perspective on pain, I began to find theological precedents all over the place. It was as if a kind of filter that had prevented theological debate around pain to take place within me was suddenly removed. The game was up. I embarked on a new exploration of the uneasy and sometimes uncomfortable territory that lies between our experience of pain and our experience of a God who loves us and who purports to be in control of his world.

Out of this emerged a new understanding, underpinned by a key principle – that pain is a part of a positive process by which we are changed. We are changed in a way that makes us more lovable to God, and hence more able to love God. Further, this process is a necessary part of the means God has chosen to complete a work of change in us, rather than an aberrant deviation from normality.

Even a cursory look at the Bible bears this out. A number of New Testament writers in particular employ images that refer to a process in which pain and suffering are key. Peter pictures a process that is like the refinement of gold:

> ...now for a little while you may have had to suffer grief in all kinds of trials. These have come so that your faith – of greater worth than gold, which perishes even though refined by fire – may be proved genuine and may result in praise, glory and honour when Jesus Christ is revealed. (1 Peter 1.6, 7)

Pain purges impurities from us, bringing those impurities to the surface where they are visible. One speaker I heard recently delved deeper into the image, drawing on his experience of seeing an Indian man purifying gold in this way. The craftsman works at the molten gold, allowing impurities to build up on the surface again and again, each time removing them without wasting any of the precious gold. He stops when he can see his face clearly in the surface of the gold in front of him. By analogy, God is the loving craftsman, deftly and gently removing our own impurities until his own image is clearly defined on the surface of ourselves.

The New Testament defines this process quite clearly. James opens his letter with these quite shocking words:

> Consider it pure joy, my brothers, whenever you face trials of many kinds, because you know that the testing of your faith develops perseverance. Perseverance must finish its work so that you may be mature and complete, not lacking anything. (James 1.2–4)

There is a quid pro quo implicit here. Pain and suffering are not just random and unfortunate consequences of a chaotic world (although they may be that too); they exist to test our faith, so that we develop perseverance. Ultimately we may be 'mature and complete, not lacking anything'. C. S. Lewis bore this out. In his reflection on his own period of intense pain he noted, 'You never know how much you really believe anything until its truth or falsehood become a matter of life and death to you.'[2] Perhaps implicit in his use of the word 'believe' is an understanding of the way Jesus used that word and the way we ought really to understand it throughout the New Testament. Jesus didn't call us to a purely cognitive belief, requiring simply that we give mental assent to a particular view of redemption. Jesus talked about a belief that impels us to new actions, new dependencies, a belief that takes up our entire person, not just the rational parts. Often it is only pain or suffering of some kind that forces a shift from one kind of belief to the other.

Paul, writing to the Romans, says, '...we also rejoice in our sufferings, because we know that suffering produces perseverance; perseverance, character; and character, hope' (Romans 5.3–4).

Rejoicing in our sufferings? This seems almost repugnant in our modern world and culture that spends inordinate amounts of time and energy avoiding those very sufferings. Rejoicing and suffering in the same sentence seems wildly oxymoronic and blatantly illogical, yet there it is. Paul, whose own experience was of persecuting and then persecution, reflects on the tangible and very logical process that the seemingly illogical experience of pain and suffering brings.

The synthesis, if there is one, to all these extracts from New Testament writers is of a very simple and ordered process unfolding out of the chaos and disorder of suffering. It works in two different dimensions: a present powerful dimension of personal change, and a more subtle one of perspective. In the first it is developing the sufferer, making them a different person, stronger, more faithful, more and more like the character of God himself. In the second the process works to propel us from the present reality of our suffering to the hope of eternity. Not in one fell swoop, or blind leap, but in a gentle process that causes us gradually to unfurl, lift our head from the mire and begin to inspect the horizon, not with dread but with hope. At the heart of the human condition, bound up in fallenness and expressed in pain and suffering of every kind, is one thing: hopelessness. And at the end of the process of regeneration and transformation that God uses to lift us from that condition is its diametric opposite, hope.

The power of pain
To me, the extraordinary thing within this divine process is that God, in order to free us from the experience of pain, does not look at the problem and seek to find some new, invented solution. Instead pain itself is employed as the key factor in the process of change. Pain acts as the catalyst, the pressure point, the critical blow that forces us away from comfort and

satisfaction to new and better places, further on and higher up. Paul Tournier talks of pain eliciting an essentially creative process in us.[3] Pain is the motivator that forces us to go beyond where we are and explore further, to engage with the innate creativity within each of us. This creativity is expressed in new questions and new solutions to the problems of the world and our experience of it. Tournier thinks of pain as a nutcracker, applying increasing pressure until the hard, impenetrable surface of the nut cracks to reveal the soft, nutritious kernel within. This process, he asserts, is inherently joy-giving. Beyond the intensity of the experience of pain, beyond the harsh transition from a place of comfort to somewhere new, is an experience of greater joy. The new place of comfort is more real and life-giving than the last.

Pain as a positive power is encapsulated in Henri Nouwen's concept of the wounded healer.[4] Nouwen draws from the life of Jesus himself, whose own pain and suffering were ultimately the powerfully positive force that brought about the possibility of transformation for human individuals. The image of Christ as a broken and wounded healer, rather than a powerful Messiah, is applied directly to the modern-day minister. In a world so full of suffering and pain the most effective means of offering or bringing about transformation is not as some powerful and patronistic bearer of healing and salvation but rather as a fellow sufferer. The distinction is in the way pain is viewed. It is not simply an enemy to be fought endlessly, a disease to be battled against. It is equally a force to be harnessed and put to use in the lives of others.

Pain and perspective

Perhaps the hardest part of the process is the dimension of time. In a culture that lives for the here and now, for the present spectacle over and above the hard won sustainable results of years of work, a process that implies a long and involved journey through pain in order to glimpse joy on the other side is not an attractive proposition. Countless industries are built on the premise that most of us would rather lose

ourselves in short-term experiences of intense, artificial joy
than face up to the possibility of change beyond the reality of
present pain.

The process we are talking about, however, factors in this
truth about the human character. Interwoven within the
process is a change in perspective that throws us out from
introspection towards a hopeful horizon. For us this was an
immediate impact. Though circumstances had changed little,
we recognized that pain was part of the process of change.
This gave us hope that we had a future and that this seemingly
endless present would in fact come to an end.

Our perspective on pain changes completely. We begin to
recognize that pain is worth enduring – in fact, not simply
endured but embraced. It is not shrunk from or shirked but
confronted, because within our understanding of pain is a
realization that this is a necessary process, beyond which is a
fuller experience of life than we have experienced before. This
dramatically new perspective doesn't run away from the
present into an unreal future. Rather it tethers the present to
a hopeful future, making the present richer. Something of the
hope and joy of the future that pain will bring flows back in
time to the present.

This brings us back to Jacob – the Jacob of Genesis and
Jacob our son. It is easy to speculate within the stories of the
Bible. Sometimes it is all we *can* do when we try to discover
how something must have felt to those involved in particular
situations. I guess now though I can feel what Jacob felt, or
at least I think I can. In the story of Jacob wrestling with the
unknown man I recognize an illustration of the process of
painful growth to joy beyond. It is an intensely human story
and the feelings seem now to flow from it as though they
were written down, rather than left to the reader's imagina-
tion. In particular Jacob's words at the heart of the story –
'I will not let you go unless you bless me' – are imbued with
determination, passion and understanding. Through spittle
and gritted teeth they say, 'This pain is not wasteful or
useless. I will not allow this pain to force me to let go of you,

there is a blessing beyond this pain and I am determined to lay claim to it.'

This is in line with the biblical Jacob's character, which is amply revealed in other stories about him. Nevertheless it demonstrates the principles behind the process of pain. Jacob has engaged with pain in wrestling with the unknown. He now confronts an intensity of pain, perhaps never felt before, because he believes that somewhere beyond the pain is something worth waiting for. Therefore I like to think that Jacob knew enough about God's character, perhaps *just* enough, to hold on when the pain of a ripped hip-joint suddenly assaulted him. He knew that this pain was not worthless; there was something in the redeeming, loving nature of God that meant he should hold on. The rumour of the God of the universe, in control and at work, was enough to make Jacob hold on for what the divine process of pain might bring.

This ought to be such an inspirational story. The fact that God is just a rumour to us is often precisely the reason we dump him in moments of pain. Wrestling with the unknown is too tough for most of us in a world that deals with problems by providing well thought through logical solutions. Yet for Jacob rumour is enough to keep him hanging in there until more of this God he believes in is revealed to him.

At the end of the process lies revelation. Revelation is an unveiling process, whereby things that were already in existence but hidden are brought into our experience for the first time. It is early days for us and our son Jacob in this process, but there are already glimmers, portents of joy and greater joy to come. While I have been working on this chapter, scared of pre-empting or overplaying what God is doing in us and Jacob through his condition, two people have independently told me of the joy they see and feel in Jacob. Jacob is an incredibly happy and joyful little boy, and he brings joy wherever he goes. For us the joy of existence is made more intense as a result of what he has been through and our awareness of what the future may hold. The present is made more precious. We rarely take life for granted when something as apparently insignificant as one single mistake in a gene can wreak such havoc. These are the beginnings of our blessing.

But let none of this detract from the fact that pain is hard, awful and unwanted. Pain is not what God wanted for his world, yet it is woven in with the deftness of a master weaver, so that pain itself might be part of the process of redemption. For us and for Jacob there are likely to be further times of wrestling – pain unwanted. Unknown men will assault us at different times and we will question their identity. No doubt in the intensity of those struggles we will turn and genuinely question whether it is a demon rather than a holy angel with whom we fight. But I hope that even within that questioning and doubt there will be enough faith in the rumour of God in us to hold on to what God may bring.

NOTES

1 Quoted in Sheila Cassidy, *Sharing the Darkness*, London: DLT 1988, p. 87.
2 C. S. Lewis, *A Grief Observed*, London: Faber and Faber 1961.
3 Paul Tournier, *Creative Suffering*, London: SCM Press 1982.
4 Henri Nouwen, *The Wounded Healer*, London: DLT 1994.

~VII~

Finally, you smile on my back
And grow into this green world
As though the joy of your face could ransack
This creation, stitched and unfurled
Belatedly for you, brought
To you more precious and more keenly un-bought.

Here we walked with you emergent,
Delayed mischievously, you 'schemer'
More than a seed then, and bent
On challenging our change forever.

And here the men with lines still wait
For wet packets of life, part-earned
By patience, part by bait
Life stagnant for a while and then returned.

~7~

Choosing Life

The kingdom of God is near. Repent and believe the good news!

Mark 1.15

... the kingdom of God is within you.

Luke 17.21

It was in writing the poems that accompany this book that I unearthed from within me the realization of what it had really meant to see Jacob get so ill and then return to health. Death had never really been an issue throughout the whole period. Jacob had never been in intensive care. He had never been at serious risk of death. Yet at another level that is exactly what it has all been about: life and death. Death had been the spectre brooding over that whole period of our lives. We had lived in its shadow, but re-emerged to find the brightness of the light of life, brightness that was much more intense for the contrast provided by the darkness of death.

This contrast between light and darkness, life and death, finds its expression in many other aspects of that whole experience. These have been explored so far in this book: faith and doubt, pain and joy, heaven and earth, present and future, hope and despair. Emerging from the whole period is an understanding of the apparent opposites around which life appears to pivot. They exist on either sides of conceptual understanding – you can even conceive of them as tilting on some kind of philosophical fulcrum – yet they are not distinct from one another. On the contrary it would seem that where modern life attempts to split them apart the designs of God are such that they are fiercely and inextricably linked. They are also linked in symbiosis, each dependent on the other, the experience of one enhanced by the other and vice versa.

Thus, through experiencing death I find life. In making space for the unknown I deepen my knowledge of God. In addressing pain I experience a new level of joy, not touched before. In wrestling with doubt I emerge with greater faith. In expressing my anger towards God I actually discover more about his love and find myself loving more. This is a pattern that exists not by chance but by design. To find more of what we seek, be it faith, life, joy, love or whatever, we are frequently forced to wrestle with its opposite.

This is ultimately a paradox. At face value it has little logic or sense to it. Only having passed through experience that showed in so many different ways that this was the case could I reflect and see a pattern at work. It would never have made sense that letting go of faith and blurting out vehement anger at God would be a way of engendering greater faith, that being willing to abandon a relationship would actually be a means of deepening it. It would never have made sense that abandoning a quest of knowing God and resting, almost belligerently, in a state of not knowing would actually impart a greater level of knowledge. This was not logical. It could not be predicted.

No wonder then that many of Jesus' statements exhibit such a baffling degree of paradox. Those who mourn will be blessed. Those last, first. The poor are rich and vice versa. The wise foolish and the foolish wise. The world is turned on its head, and nothing is as it seems. Some of Jesus' statements don't even seem to show consistency. Most notably he is recorded as making the central subject of his preaching and teaching, that is the Kingdom of God, either 'near' or 'at hand' or 'within you'. What is going on here? Is it a case of Jesus not being quite able to make up his mind? Was his message perhaps forming over time, later statements being more reliable than others? On the other hand, perhaps something so deep and so profound is going on here that it is no wonder that things seem confused. Jesus is trying to communicate some-

thing of a divine perspective and dimension into our limited
world and experience. No wonder things don't make sense;
they just don't fit.

This latter conclusion at least is where I lie. It is worth giving
the Gospel writers credit for dealing with the material that Jesus
gave them in trying to record the essence of his message and
work. Once again, if theology is to be useful it should challenge
our understanding of the world rather than conform to it.
Things do not fit. And we would be unwise to try and make
them do so simply because it makes things neater.

It seems that this quest for logical neatness still has a
pervasive and dangerous influence on people within the
Christian church. My experience of church for many years
seems on reflection to include a large amount of theological
sweeping under the carpet. In the quest for logical neatness,
for a theology with tailored edges, much of the mess and
chaos, the extra material that refuses to fit into the pattern,
gets tucked away somewhere where most of us can't see it.
Unfortunately it has a nasty habit of leaping out from the
darkness at the times we are perhaps least able to deal with it.
That is, when it is happening to us.

I feel that I was nurtured theologically on a limited but
fairly rich diet of certain faith and doctrine. This was good
stuff. I looked good – fully grown, fit, healthy. Yet underneath, vital ingredients were missing. Sterner stuff in the
skeleton of my faith was missing. Doubt, anger, death, unknowing, pain, suffering, had all been left out of the diet of
faith I had been fostered on. I was like a Christmas turkey, a
fine specimen of accelerated nurturing with little to sustain me
in the long haul of life. What teaching left out, however, the
world has forced into me. I have learnt the hard way perhaps,
forced to confront the stuff lurking in the shadows of life,
things that hadn't been pointed out to me before.

Living in two worlds
What does this have to do with Jesus' statements about the
Kingdom of God? Well, perhaps it is the failure of certain

sections of the church to grapple effectively with the ambiguity and mystery of Jesus' statements about the Kingdom that has resulted in such an expurgated version of the Christian faith being preached. More specifically, the failure of parts of the church to address the Kingdom as a present reality and instead to focus on heaven as a future goal has left gaping holes in many people's faith. It is of course unlikely that we will get a complete understanding of the profundity of Jesus' preaching on the Kingdom of God. Nevertheless we can have enough of a handle on it to make living his message more and more real and powerful in the world we currently inhabit.

This is after all what it is about. Worlds. Or more specifically, two of them. Two worlds coexisting, the present one and the future one. One is the world of our general experience, the one that involves the road outside and the tree in the garden, the train to work and the post in the morning. The other is the domain of God, the Kingdom of God, where the presence of God fully dwells and where the outflowing of that presence in all its many dimensions affects everything.

Jesus came saying that this Kingdom was now, here; you couldn't see it but it was here. It existed within its subjects and therefore remained invisible but there would come a time when it would be fully revealed, visibly and physically. It also permeated this world. It wasn't that the worlds were split apart, except for the odd excursion of one into another. No, in one sense the two worlds are like warp and woof, inseparable. It is as Hopkins says: the 'world is charged with the glory of God'.[1] Yet in another sense they are distinct, separated perhaps not physically but by perception. It is we who separate one from the other by our relative inability to see the Kingdom in our midst. Yet there would be a time when we would see the Kingdom more clearly. In fact, that is all we would see, for all would be revealed in its fullness. So the Kingdom of God is both here now and yet also near and somewhere in the future.

It is this doctrine of coexistence that causes the problem. For some parts of the church it is as though we can live in the full experience of the Kingdom of God now: we can experience it now because of Jesus. We can somehow slough off the old skin of our world and live in little bubbles of heaven, hermetically sealed from the world. Sadly this can lead to huge disappointment and often damage. Living triumphantly in the fullness of the Kingdom when the realities of the world break in, for example in the tragic death of a loved one or a disease that refuses to respond to faithful prayer, frequently leads to the breaking of many people's faith.

On the other hand, other parts of the church find the notion of the presence of the Kingdom of God in the present world difficult: faith is reduced to an essentially cognitive process of belief. We rationally assent to the message of Jesus and this gives us access to the Kingdom in the future when we die. The emphasis on rational faith then leads to a gospel with the messy parts overlooked, for fear of unsettling what is most important.

These are oversimplifications, but they highlight a great sadness: that much of the present-day church is living in a skewed understanding of the gospel that Jesus himself taught. Jesus used the word 'repent' not to mean that we should simply turn from our sin and get ourselves morally and spiritually prepared for the Kingdom. He meant 'repent' in the sense of taking on a completely new way of living, there and then. Jesus' gospel called its disciples to live a life with one foot in the Kingdom and the other in the world, holding both in tension. He called them to live a life that therefore grappled with the secondary tensions that then arose: tensions between death and life, pain and joy, darkness and light.

Choosing the Kingdom

Ultimately Jesus offered his potential followers a choice. He suggested that they choose to take up a citizenship in the Kingdom of God while remaining for a time very much citizens of earth. They would be fully paid up and effective citizens of heaven while getting their feet covered in the dust of the earth. And each and every day they would have to continue to make that choice. On waking up each day the citizen of heaven asks, 'Do I today choose to live in the Kingdom of God, that exists even though I cannot see it, or choose to live in the world?' We continue to ask this question. The ultimate choice between one world and another is made not just once but many times. Indeed, as many times as there are days since we made that choice for the very first time.

An understanding of the Kingdom of God as a world coexisting alongside our physical world forces us to confront the tough things of life. The world throws up its situations and the question remains, 'Do I choose to live in the Kingdom in this situation, and if so how?' This book is really a record of that question, asked over and over again in us as we went through the whole period of our son becoming seriously ill and eventually recovering. We were forced to be creative, delving into parts of the Bible that for some reason had been quietly avoided before. We were forced to express things to God that had seemed tantamount to blasphemy before, and forced to question some of the very basics of faith, such as prayer.

Frequently the world throws up alternatives that provide us with a blatant choice between the Kingdom and the present world. In the midst of undeserved suffering we are therefore given a choice between a God bigger and less knowable than we thought or, to take the world's view, no God at all or quite frankly a malevolent one. In the midst of unanswered prayer we are offered a choice between a God who perhaps has something more life-giving in store for us or, to take the world's view, a God who is either arbitrary or deaf.

Perhaps the best way to illustrate this is with a more up-to-date example from our life with Jacob's condition. Jacob has cystic fibrosis. It is a genetic condition inherited very simply. Emily and I are carriers and each time we conceive a child we give one of two copies of the CF gene. This could be a good copy or bad copy, a 'healthy' copy or a CF copy. It takes a little working out, but the simple outcome is that once Emily and I decided we wanted to have children, the chances of Jacob having CF were one in four. The same is true of any further children. Of course, with Jacob we were unaware of these odds, but since having him we are forced to consider them. Each time we conceive a child we 'throw the dice' and run a 25 per cent risk of our child having CF.

Understandably for some this proves enough to make them decide to stick rather than twist. However, we were willing to take the risk. Some months after taking this decision Emily became pregnant.

Then we had another choice, indeed a number of choices. The first was whether we wanted to test early on for CF. New technology means that very early in the pregnancy cells can be removed and tested for the presence of good or bad copies of the gene. The world presented us with a choice: 'Would you like to see if this child has CF and if so, dispense with it and try again?' This was for us an easy choice: termination, even at an early stage, was not an option.

The second choice was harder. At any time up to 32 weeks we could test the amniotic fluid and so find out whether or not the baby had CF. Another alternative was to take blood from the umbilical cord at birth, and this would be sent for testing. In medical terms we could choose to know the CF status of our child either some months before birth or three weeks after. This also seemed a simple choice: we had been through the agony of not knowing and it seemed sensible, and surely kind to ourselves, to minimize that tension and anxiety this time. However, for whatever reason, we delayed deciding about the amniocentesis for some time.

Returning to the subject a few weeks later, we realized that doubts had crept in. There is always a small risk of miscarriage with an amniocentesis and perhaps that coloured our thinking. We began to think again. Until then we had considered this choice primarily on medical grounds (what was best clinically?), or in terms of how we would be affected emotionally (what was the route of least anxiety?). Then we asked a different question. What does everything we learnt through our experience of Jacob's illness say about this decision? This took us into another level of discussion.

Through Jacob's illness we had learnt a great many things. Perhaps most applicable to this situation was learning the benefits of resting in the unknown. In the many periods of unknowing during Jacob's illness we had recognized a space that required simple dependence on God. This space was beyond rational understandings of God and his ways; it was space where you and God simply dwelt together. Job went there, and came back exclaiming, 'Surely I spoke of things I did not understand, things too wonderful for me to know' (Job 42.3). This was a place where a true understanding of God's sovereignty and greatness could be learnt and where our lack of understanding and need for God is laid bare.

Were we willing to re-enter that space? It seemed in some ways unnecessary. Others may not do what we did, not because they choose wrong but because they choose differently. We could have taken what modern medical science – the same science that might well find a cure for Jacob – had to offer and know the fate of our second child in time for us to adjust to whatever it was. Yet that seemed wrong to us. We were compelled to re-enter the unknown and throw ourselves into the all-knowing and loving arms of God.

The story of the Jewish people, from the point where they are given their identity as the people of God to the return from exile, is similarly a story about a people forever having to make choices between a God they cannot see and the alternatives thrown up by the world. Sometimes the option suggested by God seems at best illogical and at worst suicidal. Joshua decides to take the city of Jericho by marching seemingly harmlessly seven times round the walls and then blowing on a few trumpets. Gideon decides to fight the Midianites heavily outnumbered, with an army reduced from 32,000 to 300 men.

In another story the Israelites decide that there is a choice to be made between being led by a king or being led by God (1 Samuel 8). This story has become particularly pertinent to us because it shows the people of God making a choice between the unknown and invisible way of God and the very visible and apparently sensible way of the world. 'Give us a

king to lead us,' the Israelites say to Samuel. Samuel argues
that a king will be a harsh ruler, doing as he pleases, dictating
over them. Still the Israelites argue for a king, saying most
significantly, 'We shall be like all the other nations, with a king
to lead us and to go out before us and fight our battles' (1
Samuel 8.20).

This is what all the other nations have and it seems to work
– a king going out before them to fight their battles for them.
Why should Israel be any different? The world suggests a
solution that is both sensible and proven to be successful. Why
shouldn't it work for the people of God? Well, sometimes it
does. In the case of a king for Israel God relents, and within
the line of kings of Israel there are enough successes to suggest
that maybe it worked. Yet you can't help feeling that this was
not the best for Israel, the people of God, chosen to be a people
under the direction and rule of God.

This story convinced us further that we were to make the
choice that we did. The world presented us with a sensible and
perfectly reasonable route, but we would take the way that we
felt God was offering us, into the unknown, dependent on his
direction and his ways. As I write we still do not know whether
or not our baby daughter, born nearly three weeks ago, has
CF. It has not been easy. We swing from one conclusion to
another. She cries all night, as Jacob did, and we conclude that
we have been 'unlucky' again. She puts on weight in her first
week, something Jacob failed to do, and we conclude that she
is free from this condition. Yet ultimately we do not know and
that forces us to see her not as a child with or without CF but
as purely a child, made in the image of God and with the
character of God imprinted upon her. She has been allowed at
the very least a precious three weeks without CF colouring our
perception of her.

Meanwhile in our watching and waiting within the unknown we have found once again the uncluttered space
beyond the world. We have not been bothered by medical
interventions, which though rationally defensible would have
served only to give us knowledge sooner rather than later.

Sometimes knowledge is nothing more than noise that fills the quiet space in which God dwells. Without that knowledge we are able to dwell there too in silence.

In the middle

If I conclude anything from our experience of Jacob's illness it is this: it is not unusual, rather it is perfectly normal. For what we experienced was an intensification, in time and in form, of all our experience of living in this world, of being caught in the coexistence of two worlds and waiting for the fullness of one to be released by the dissipation of the other. As Philip Yancey puts it in reference to another intensification episode, that of Lazarus:

> All of us live out our days in the in-between time, the interval of chaos and confusion between Lazarus' death and reappearance. Although such a time may be temporary, and may pale into insignificance alongside the glorious future that awaits us, right now it is all we know, and that is enough to bring tears to our eyes...[2]

Our suffering, our pain, our waiting in the unknown for God to show up is not unusual. This is the reality of the time we live in, the messy chaotic space in the middle between one world and the next, where we feel the painful consequences of one and yet the tantalizing sweet succour of the next. This coexistence of apparent opposites is hard. In some ways it would be easier not to know that a world free of all the pain and suffering of this one were so agonizingly close. This was the pain that even Jesus felt as he stood before the tomb of the dead Lazarus, fully aware of his ability to resurrect him, yet fully aware of the pain of death. That the separation between death and life for Lazarus was so slim served only to illustrate how slim it was for the rest of the world. This moved him to tears, such was the intensity of that moment.

We all live in that moment. A moment infused with pain and yet with the potential for so much joy. A moment that balances on outrageous paradoxes, irrational opposites. A moment that has at its heart the ultimate expression of the fallenness of the world we live in. A moment that is but another moment from resurrection and the triumph over death.

But the question that permeates unspoken throughout this book is this: how many of us remove ourselves in some way from that moment, where all the pain and joy to be had in this world is intensified and held together in tension? How many of us purport to live in the Kingdom and yet are afraid to grapple with the essential challenges it throws up? How many people live with a lesser experience of the Kingdom of God because they are unable to stand at the tomb of Lazarus and confront the tension inherent between this world and the next?

We were forced into that moment. In that tomb lay not Lazarus but Jacob, our son, and we like Jesus cried the tears of pain mixed with joy as Jacob re-emerged and rediscovered life. In the chaos and intensity of that moment we held on to faith, on to the existence and sovereignty of God. Others do not; they lose faith, or turn away, hide their eyes, dive into the crowd of mourners and watch from a distance. By the grace of God we got through that extended moment, not through any heroism of faith restricted or unavailable to anyone else. We survived through the support of others who were faith for us. We got through because we kept asking questions, often full of doubt and anger but all holding the reality of God as a given. There was for us enough of a rumour of God to believe that there was more of him to be found on the other side of our pain, so we held on.

The truth is that God allows such moments to form us and mould us – to develop faith, not destroy it. By shirking them we remove ourselves from God's means of generating greater faith, joy and relationship with him in the Kingdom of God. We cannot create these moments ourselves. But when they come along, how we respond to them is crucial. This is the choice. There is a question to answer: 'Do I choose to live in the Kingdom of God in this situation, and if so how?' That question is asked over and over again in both the easy times and the 'Lazarus moments', when the reality of our coexistence intensifies so much we can feel it. In asking that question we confront rather than shirk the challenges of the Kingdom. In asking that question over and over again we begin to experience the paradox of life in the middle, where joy is found through pain, faith through doubt, stillness through anger and ultimately life through death.

NOTES

1 Gerard Manley Hopkins, 'God's Grandeur', *Poems and Prose*, Harmondsworth: Penguin 1985.
2 Philip Yancey, *The Jesus I Never Knew*, London: HarperCollins 1999, p. 180.

Afterword

It is important to say that in one sense there is never an ending. To 'end' a book about suffering and about the blurred edges of our understanding where real faith is forged is almost paradoxical. There is no end word. We keep exploring, we keep asking questions.

As I write I am aware that we have by no means reached the end of our journey with Jacob. At present we are living in the chaotic fun of having two young children. We also live in the relief and thankfulness that Bethany does not have CF. Strangely, though, these feelings come tinged with sadness as they reinforce within our own home the reality of the misfortune that Jacob has to suffer. For him, almost certainly, there will be times of suffering and pain. Cystic fibrosis is a degenerative condition. Jacob's lungs will not always be as good as they are now. Of course, there is the hope of a cure: of all the genetic conditions that affect people chronically CF is perhaps the one with the greatest hope of being beaten. However, we cannot rely on a cure being found, or being found in time. In the meantime Jacob will fight and we will fight. Sometimes we will win, but gradually, with things as they stand, we are likely to lose.

Within that reality there are some truths. Pain and suffering are horrible. Sometimes theologizing pain can take the sting out of it. Sometimes books like this leave you divorced from the intense experience of pain by the persuasiveness of their theory. It is all very well to say that pain is there to mould us towards a greater faith and deeper faith in God, but these remain tough words for the person in the midst of pain. As much as we recognize the extraordinary ways in which God is able to work through pain, we would still much rather that Jacob was free of it. This is ultimately at the heart of what God wants to bring about in our world, a place where there will 'never again be ... an infant who lives but a few days' or where there are children who are born 'doomed to misfortune' (Isaiah 65.20, 23).

And of course there is the real and wonderful potential for healing. We continue to hold on to the truth that God can and does perform miraculous acts of healing. He may well do this for Jacob and for us. We press into that possibility fully aware that it may or may not happen and willing to struggle faithfully in the event that it does not.

I visit a man in his nineties once every fortnight or so for a cup of tea. As I come through the door we exchange greetings. These greetings have now developed into an amusing and poignant mantra. 'How are you?' he says to me. 'Fine', I say. 'How's the family?' 'Well, thank you', I reply. Pause. 'And how are you?' I say. To which he always replies, 'Oh, struggling, struggling.'

The more I drink an infrequent cup of tea with this lovely man the more I realize that we struggle and we struggle. When we think we have solved things and the struggle is over, we struggle some more. This man, heading for a century, knows struggle more than me, and that humbles and inspires me. We will continue to struggle, but not without hope. In that way we will continue to struggle.